PERSPECTIVES
ON
ECONOMIC
GROWTH

Perspectives
ON
Economic
Growth

EDITED BY

Walter·W·Heller

RANDOM HOUSE

NEW YORK

FIRST PRINTING
© Copyright, 1968, by Walter W. Heller
All rights reserved under International and Pan-
American Copyright Conventions. Published in
New York by Random House, Inc., and simultane-
ously in Toronto, Canada, by Random House of
Canada, Limited. Manufactured in the United
States of America. Designed by Vincent Torre.

Library of Congress catalog card number: 66-11981

To
JOHN F. KENNEDY
Who initiated and inspired this volume

What is at stake in our economic decisions today is not some grand warfare of rival ideologies which will sweep the country with passion but the practical management of a modern economy. What we need is not labels and clichés but more basic discussion of the sophisticated and technical questions involved in keeping a great economic machinery moving ahead.

The national interest lies in high employment and steady expansion of output, in stable prices, and a strong dollar. The declaration of such an objective is easy; their attainment in an intricate and interdependent economy and world is a little more difficult. To attain them, we require not some automatic response but hard thought.

PREFACE

The present collection of essays had its origins in the Washington of John F. Kennedy. The nation's lagging growth rate and frequent recessions had been the prime campaign issues in the 1960 election. Indeed, the first question Kennedy ever put to me—during a chance encounter in October 1960—went like this: "Do you think we can make good on that 5 percent growth promise in the Democratic platform?" The need to "get the country moving again" remained at the center of the Kennedy Administration's concern after it took office.

Simultaneously with short-term programs aimed at turning recession into recovery, new programs to generate faster productivity growth were launched—manpower training and development programs, along with requests for enactment of new tax incentives for plant and equipment investment.

Constrained by the limits of public and congressional economic understanding, yet perceiving the potency of modern economic policy, President Kennedy increasingly committed the nation to an active economic policy, with specific national objectives in mind. That commitment went well beyond a limited and intermittent concern with extremes of the business cycles to a widespread and continual concern with the economy's performance —with its performance not only in fulfilling but in expanding its productive potential.

Because its achievement would aid in the pursuit of many other goals, faster economic growth became a central objective of the new government policies. Measures to expand total demand and output were the key to restoring full employment. But faster expansion of our full-employment potential required more. Here, the key was to be found in larger investments in brainpower and skills, in research and technology, and in modern plant and equipment. And the resulting rapid productivity growth would also help maintain price stability and the competitive position of American products in world markets.

These have been some of the broad premises of economic policy since 1961. How to translate them into specific policy prescriptions and gain public acceptance for these prescriptions have been among the important tasks challenging economists in recent years. Fresh and imaginative analysis has been required and forthcoming. So has an understanding and understandable presentation of the analysis and its implications.

In his continuous desire to raise the level of dialogue on economic questions, President Kennedy had encouraged publication of a volume of essays that would provide an unconstrained discussion of economic growth as a national objective. The present volume is descendant from those days and that idea, although it is somewhat broader in coverage than those beginnings might suggest. It goes beyond a discussion of specific issues and proposals to include contributions reflecting the present state of economic research on many aspects of the growth question.

George Perry opens the volume with an examination of the overall implications and responsibilities of a national commitment to growth. His chapter introduces the other essays in this volume. Arthur Okun discusses quantitative stabilization policies and the role of the 1964 tax cut in the present expansion. Warren Smith analyzes how coordinated fiscal and monetary policies can aim for both stabilization and growth goals. James Tobin (in an essay which is reprinted here, with only slight revisions, through the courtesy of the editor of the *American Economic Review,* in which it first appeared in December 1964) explores the question of how much growth we should strive for and why the government must concern itself with the question at all. Richard Cooper examines the implications for growth policy of our foreign trade position and foreign aid responsibilities and finds some specific national considerations for encouraging growth. Robert Lampman evaluates the benefits to individual welfare that have resulted from our past growth. Three of the authors, William Bowen, Richard Nelson, and Robert Solow, analyze how we can affect our growth rate and explore the importance of both tangible investment in factories and machines and intangible investment in research, education, and other forms of human betterment, as sources of economic growth.

Each contributor to the present volume is a prominent professional economist. Several of them are specialists in economic theory who have made major analytical contributions to the theory of economic growth. All of them have had Washington experience as economists at the Council of Economic Advisers or elsewhere.

This collection of their essays is not meant to present conflicting sides of various issues, as collected selections of readings frequently do. Rather, it is meant as a presentation of the latest thinking and findings along the mainstream of professional economic thought on the broad question of economic growth.

The state of the economy today testifies clearly to the need for an active and flexible policy. Just as some were beginning to cry that this generation of economic advisers knew only how to seek expansion and stimulus for the economy, the Vietnam war imposed its demands on an economy already nearing its optimal operating point—and these same economists were the first to insist on the need for restrictive policies. In an economy that will more consistently be operating in the neighborhood of its productive potential, the need to be flexible, to be ready to restrain as well as to stimulate in response to short-term development, will be increasingly important.

But what of the general trends of future policy? I think some guidelines for carrying out our commitment to growth have become clear. The restored investment tax credit and provisions for accelerated depreciation are an important element in our program for growth. Similarly, our long-run interests in encouraging investment and modernization will call for policies to bring interest rates considerably below their current high levels once the domestic and international economic pressures of the Vietnam war are behind us. And, combining our desire to invigorate the *sources* of growth with our concern that its bounty be put to the proper *uses,* growth policy will call for ever-larger investment, not just in our national physical capital—including public investment in natural resources, transportation, pollution control, and urban rebirth—but in the health, education, and training of our people.

One of the challenging issues of our time will be how to provide for our needs in these areas through combinations of direct Federal programs, tax changes that encourage activity by the private sector, and new initiatives for expanding the traditional role of state and local governments. If this volume offers—as I believe it does—some useful perspectives on the nature of the growth process, on what is at stake, and on the policies that can meet our growth objectives, it will make its contribution to a vital dialogue.

WALTER W. HELLER

February, 1968

CONTENTS

Part I

Growth and Economic Policy

BY

George L. Perry

INTRODUCTION

In most countries economic growth has for a long time been the number one objective of government economic policy. By contrast, in the modern-day United States growth has become a conscious object of policy only recently. The start of an official U.S. commitment to growth may be marked in 1961, with our participation in the twenty-nation Organization for Economic Cooperation and Development agreement to aim for a collective 50 percent growth in output over the decade of the 1960's. And in the perspective of the times, this was an ambitious commitment: If we were to meet the twenty-nation average, we would have to achieve a sharply faster advance than the 37 percent output gain achieved between 1950 and 1960. In January 1962, the Council of Economic Advisers devoted a chapter of its Annual Report to economic growth. In subsequent reports, the Council has repeatedly discussed the role of government policies in this area. Today, with the rising interest of economists in the study of economic growth and with the rising prominence of economists in government policy-making, continuing attention to growth as a policy objective seems assured.

ECONOMIC EXPANSION

The rapid and uninterrupted expansion of output since 1961 has made growth popular and has raised expectations about how well the United States' economy can perform. Yet this experience can be quite misleading.

In the analytical models of economists, a strong distinction is drawn between "pure" economic growth and the more general phenomenon of economic expansion. The 1961–65 period started with high unemployment and excess industrial capacity. We had the economic potential to produce $40 to $50 billion more Gross National Product in 1961 simply by putting obviously idle resources to work. Therefore policy during the period correctly had as its first concern the elimination of this economic slack through promotion of a sufficiently strong economic expansion. And it succeeded: real national output in the United States grew by 22.5 percent between 1961 and 1965, a measure of the economic expansion over the period. But the growth of economic potential, the operational equivalent of pure economic growth, was only an estimated 15 percent. Once the economy achieves full employment, as it now has in 1966, the rate of further economic expansion is limited by the growth in potential GNP.

Growth policy thus comes to the fore in the fully employed economy. This is when we must give up some of one good if we are to get more of another. And this is what a policy on growth rates must be all about: how much of current production is to be invested for the future and how much is to be consumed now. Yet the prior requirement is for stabilization policies that maintain full employment. The discrepancy between actual and potential GNP that existed in 1961 was no isolated observation. Cyclical fluctuations are found throughout our economic history. And the existence of a substantial gap between our potential and actual output in a given year has characterized recent economic performance all too often, as Table 1 shows. There a breakdown is given of the changes in actual GNP, changes in estimated potential GNP, and changes in the gap between potential and actual, together with the size of the gap, for each year since the Korean War.

The changes in potential GNP represent what I have called

TABLE 1

Actual GNP and GNP Gaps
1958 Prices (in billions of dollars)

(Changes are from preceding year)

	1955	1956	1957	1958	1959	1960	1961	1962	1963	1964	1965
Change in actual GNP	+31	+8	+6.5	−5	+27.5	+12	+9.5	+32.5	+21	+29	+34.5
Change in potential GNP	+15	+15.5	+16	+16.5	+17	+17.5	+18	+19	+20.5	+21.5	+22.5
Change in GNP gap	−16	+7	+9.5	+21.5	−11	+5.5	+8.5	−13.5	−1	−7	−12
Size of gap	1	8	17.5	39	28	33.5	42	28.5	27.5	20.5	8.5

TABLE 2

Business Fixed Investment and GNP Gaps

	Investment as % of potential GNP	GNP gap as % of actual GNP
1954	8.8	4.1
1955	9.6	0.2
1956	10.3	1.4
1957	10.1	3.9
1958	8.6	8.8
1959	8.8	5.8
1960	9.0	6.9
1961	8.3	8.5
1962	8.8	5.3
1963	8.8	5.0
1964	9.3	3.5
1965	10.1	1.4

pure growth. If, as a result of growth measures taken at the start of the period, the rate of pure growth had been 10 percent greater in each following year than it is estimated to have been, potential output in 1965 would have been greater by $20 billion (in 1958 prices). Over the whole post-Korean period, this change in the pure growth rate would have added $96 billion of potential GNP (the sum of what would have been added to potential in each year of the period). This is an impressive addition, and it would have required an impressive sacrifice of present consumption in each year, as we shall see later. By comparison, if actual GNP had equaled the potential actually estimated in each of these years (an ideal of stabilization policy that could not literally be achieved) $271 billion of additional GNP would have been produced over this period (the sum of the gaps estimated for each year). This is an even more impressive addition, and no offsetting sacrifice would have been required.

But it is not just this kind of comparison that makes attention to the growth of actual output a prior requirement to policies for pure growth. It is also that successful full-employment policies encourage the rapid growth of potential while economic slack and recession discourage it. The existence of idle capacity discourages new business investment. Skills deteriorate with unemployment. And the learning process from which new technology springs is slowed. Had full employment been maintained over the past decade, the growth of potential GNP would have been faster through these effects alone.

That an important connection does exist between business investment spending and economic slack, as measured by the GNP gap, is clear from Table 2. (There is, of course, causation running the other way as well; the stronger is investment demand, the smaller will the GNP gap be, other things equal. By relating investment to immediately previous percentage gaps as well as to current gaps in the table, this other effect is minimized.) This and some of the other connections between full employment and pure growth are amplified by other authors in this volume.

FISCAL AND MONETARY POLICIES

There is reason to think that the stabilization–full-employment record will be better in the future. Arthur Okun's paper specifically analyzes the part that the 1964 tax reductions played in the present sustained expansion to full employment. By implication, it also shows that our quantitative understanding of the economy's operation has reached the point where policy can aim for the full-employment target with some precision. In planning the tax cut, the employment target was translated into a required increment to total output and demand. The policy changes needed to bring forth this much demand were estimated from what was known of the behavior of consumers and businesses. And the results were very much what economists had expected they would be. The successes of recent years have made clear to the public what has been clear to the economist for some time: We can keep the economy operating at or near its potential and reduce the frequency and severity of economic downturns far better than we have been.

What is more, policy can aim to meet a growth target while keeping its primary orientation to the maintenance of full employment. To grow faster, the U.S. economy would have to invest more and consume less out of a given total level of output. Now a continuous range of fiscal and monetary policy combinations are capable of maintaining total output at the full-employment level. While at a given time each combination thus leads to the same GNP, they differ in the mix of consumption and investment spending in the total. Warren Smith's paper explores how coordinated fiscal and monetary policies can be used to get both the desired total output level *and* the desired mix.

Basically, taxes must reduce purchasing power to free resources that would otherwise be used for producing consumer goods; at the same time, investment expenditures must be large enough to utilize the freed resources. Monetary policy can encourage investment expenditures by maintaining low interest rates, thus increasing the net expected return from potential investment projects. In addition, direct and indirect stimulants to investment can be provided through the tax system, and public investment spending can be increased directly.

The single most useful measure of what fiscal policy is doing is the full-employment budget surplus (or deficit)— that is, the estimated difference between revenues and expenditures that would exist if the economy were operating at full employment and generating the corresponding incomes. To a first approximation, the position of monetary policy can be summarized by the (average) level of interest rates. In general, policy combinations involving larger full-employment budget surpluses and lower interest rates are the more conducive of economic growth. But this is an imperfect guide. If specific tax incentives to investment are used or if more public investment is undertaken, we could be moving toward a more growth-oriented policy without any increase in the full-employment budget surplus; it would depend on what other demands were suppressed and by what means. Finally, when policy acts both to stimulate expansion, because the economy is operating well below full employment, and to encourage growth of potential, it may have to encourage investment *and* consumption rather than investment at the expense of consumption. Here a reduction in the full-employment budget surplus may well be the only practical way to achieve both ends. This point is well illustrated by what happened in the first half of the 1960's.

Between the end of 1960 and the end of 1965, the full-employment budget surplus was lowered from about $14 billion to about zero through a series of tax and expenditure changes. The large full-employment surplus of 1960 would have left room for very large investment levels at full employment. But the required investment demand was not forthcoming. (It is hard to say whether a substantially easier monetary policy alone could have raised investment demand enough; in fact, interest rates were kept high because of balance-of-payments difficulties.)

Table 3 shows the fiscal measures taken in this period. Because the output and incomes associated with full employment grow through time, full-employment revenues and the potential budget surplus would grow accordingly were it not for offsets in the form of expenditure increases or tax reductions. The first entry in the table shows that potential revenue growth would have added $34 billion to the budget surplus over the five-year period; in addition, payroll tax changes would have added $3 billion more. The rest of the categories shown added up to $51 billion of surplus reduction.

Included in the surplus-reducing measures were several that were oriented toward investment stimulus and growth.

TABLE 3

*Factors Changing the Full-Employment Budget Surplus
Second Half 1960 to Second Half 1965*

(in billions of dollars)

Revenue Changes

Full-employment revenue growth (at constant tax rates)	+34
Payroll tax changes	+ 3
Indirect business tax changes	− 2
Corporate tax changes	− 6
Personal income tax changes	−11
SUBTOTAL	+18

Expenditure Changes

Defense purchases	− 6
Space program purchases	− 5
Domestic nondefense purchases	− 3
Grants-in-aid	− 5
Personal transfers	− 9
Interest and subsidy payments	− 4
SUBTOTAL	−32
TOTAL: Net change in full-employment surplus	−14

The $6 billion of corporate tax reduction fits in this category. And of this total, the $3-billion reduction in the form of more generous depreciation provisions for tax purposes and direct tax credits for investment in new equipment were specially potent. Although aimed primarily at expanding consumption, the $11-billion personal tax reduction included important incentives to investment and risk-taking as well by providing large reductions in the highest marginal tax rates and introducing income averaging.

GROWTH OF POTENTIAL

If, in the past five years, we have had some easy acceleration in our economic expansion by lowering unemployment and moving up to our economic potential, we can now look forward to some easy acceleration in our pure growth rate.

The postwar babies are reaching working age; and for the next decade the potential labor force is expected to increase by an average of nearly 2 percent annually—roughly one-half percentage point faster than in the preceding decade. If output per man rises no faster than before, our growth rate will move to around 4 percent a year from the roughly 3.5 percent-a-year average growth in potential estimated for the 1955–65 period.

But the growth that comes from an expanding labor force and an average increment to productivity is what we may call the natural growth rate. When we go beyond this, the real questions of stimulating growth appear: whether to accelerate (or slow down) the growth that would come naturally, and how to do so if we decide to.

WHY STRESS GROWTH?

The Socially Optimal Time Path. James Tobin's paper addresses the particularly difficult question of how much growth we should strive for. It is clear that economics alone cannot settle the matter. At bottom it is one of those choices a society must make, involving a selection of less of one thing and more of another—in this case, the selection between the amount of consumption at different points in time. Tobin argues that society is really expressing a choice for faster growth than our market economy is providing.

The rate of return on investment represents the terms on which society can gain further output by postponing current consumption and using the resources for current investment instead. The rate of return available to savers represents the time preference of society, the amount of additional consumption they must be able to get in the future if they are willing to forego some consumption today. Optimality is achieved when enough saving and investment is undertaken to bring the social return to investment even with society's time preference: The last dollar invested yields just enough to warrant the last dollar of saving that made it possible.

Tobin explains why the economy's market forces alone are unlikely to make the optimal choice, and why government policy cannot expect to be neutral on the issue. He cites a number of reasons why the social returns to more investment probably exceed the returns available to private savers, and why, therefore, the social payoff in greater future consumption would justify its cost in more consumption foregone today. Because of factors such as differences between social and private risk, the inability of individual investors to capture all the social returns to investment, and the existence of important market imperfections, Tobin reasons we are investing too little of our output to satisfy our own tastes and preferences. Calculations in this area still rest on inadequate information and excessive assumptions. But Tobin's arguments are ingenious and persuasive. They are likely to be the starting points of future discussions for some time to come.

Some National Motives for Growth. Richard Cooper's paper introduces international considerations to the growth question. He discusses the interrelations between domestic growth and our balance of payments. And he presents the case for faster growth as an aid in pursuit of our international aims and our role of world leadership. These pursuits involve essentially social rewards. They may be justified by important externalities, very long-run and widespread returns which would not motivate sufficient private effort. In this connection, he cites three types of advantage to be gained from more rapid economic growth in the United States: A greater national income would make it easier to provide aid to the less developed nations and to meet other inherently national demands on our output. It would aid these nations indirectly as well by enlarging our demands for their products. And it would enhance the prestige of our nation and the attractiveness of our system compared with the socialist alternative.

The growth (and expansion) of the first half of this decade

have already yielded some very specific benefits in a context noted both by Cooper and Tobin—enlarging our capacity to meet national emergencies. Tobin notes that the availability of a large economic potential in time of war can be viewed as but another case of the standard growth-decision equation: whether, in the future, a war's demands will be met entirely from the foregone consumption of the moment and the future; or whether, by past investments which enlarge total productive capacity, achieved through foregone past consumption, they may be spread backward in time as well. Today, the demands of the Vietnam war are being met with only the mildest restraints on current production for other purposes. Because of the long and sustained surge of business investment that started in 1963, adequate industrial capacity is available. With unemployment at 4 percent in the first quarter of 1966, average operating rates in manufacturing were estimated between 90 percent and 91 percent, still below preferred rates of 92 percent.

Growth and Individual Welfare. At bottom, we seek economic growth because of what it can do for people. In his essay, Robert Lampman concerns himself with how growth affects human welfare and how we can gauge the benefits of growth from available data. He takes note of the diseconomies that growth may involve and of the need to consider the distribution of benefits from growth as well as the changing aggregates. As a first approximation to the change in welfare, Lampman settles on the change in real per capita consumption, including the collective consumption of goods and services provided by the government. Yet when it comes to actual measurement, he notes important ambiguities in even this straightforward measure: The value of new products resulting from innovation and discovery cannot be reflected properly in consumption data; to a lesser extent, the same is true of all quality changes in final goods. On the other hand, the recorded increase in consumption that reflects a shift from home production to market purchases overstates the gain involved.

And more generally, consumption increases required to offset the disadvantages of growth and change should not be included as welfare gains. The need to spend more on commuting as urban congestion worsens is a clear example.

Some of these difficulties, and others as well, are encompassed in Lampman's reminder that growth involves change and that this will suit some more than others. American society today is hardly just a more prosperous blowup of society fifty years ago. Lampman examines the balance sheet of changes and concludes that our past growth has been beneficial, that the costs experienced were more than offset by the gains. He notes that the growth in consumption during the postwar years has been accompanied by more leisure, more wealth, more income security, and a lower incidence of poverty, all signs of well-being that tend to confirm the growth of per capita income as a rough indicator of improved welfare.

INDIVIDUAL FACTORS
AFFECTING GROWTH

When it comes to analyzing the specific elements of the growth process—what use should we make of the resources released when we forego consumption today—economic measurement is again in its infancy. We know that business investment in physical capital makes workers more productive. We know that outlays on research and development help make newer methods and machines more efficient than older ones. We know, too, that highly educated men are best equipped to produce technical innovations, that considerable education is useful even to operate a technically advanced facility, and that some education is helpful in almost any job. We know that good health increases the efficiency of individual workers and increases total efficiency even more by reducing absenteeism. We know that public investment is as crucial in the growth equation as private investment.

What we are only beginning to know is, how much? As a nation, we not only choose how much of our present output to save and invest for future gain, but how much of our total investment to channel into each alternative form. This comes down to comparing what the future payoff is to investing an additional dollar today in each of the alternatives open to us.

This type of rate-of-return calculation is continually being made throughout our economy and implicitly or explicitly governs many of our decisions. A firm decides whether to buy an additional machine or expand its research staff. A young man decides whether to get a Master's degree. A community debates whether to build a new elementary school. Many of these decisions are make in the normal workings of our market economy; others, by their nature, involve the political process as well. In either case, if appropriate decisions are to be made in all these areas, national policy must judge the social costs and returns, and influence the outcomes accordingly.

Three of the authors in the present volume, William Bowen, Richard Nelson, and Robert Solow, address themselves to some of these separate factors influencing the rate of economic growth—to some of the major kinds of investment that a society undertakes.

Plant and Equipment. Solow deals primarily with what may be called "tangible" investment, describing investment that adds to the physical stock of plant and equipment, as distinguished from "intangible" investment, typlified by devoting resources to research, education, and health—areas discussed by Nelson and Bowen. Solow distinguishes three effects of adding to our physical capital. The first is "capital widening," the process of adding plant and machinery in pace with increases in employment. In isolation, this process keeps the average amount of (unchanging) physical capital used with each worker constant through time. The second effect is "capital deepening," the process of increasing the amount of (unchanging) physical capital used with each worker. The third effect is "capital quickening," the process of improving the average quality of capital used with each worker.

In using these categories, Solow notes that widening increases total capacity in line with employment growth, leaving labor productivity unaffected; deepening increases capacity by increasing labor productivity, but is subject to diminishing returns to capital and declining profitability on new investment; while quickening raises productivity and makes possible the deepening of capital without declining profitability.

This way of looking at the role of investment also explains the theoretical conclusion that in the *very* long run, the rate of growth turns out to depend entirely on labor force growth and technical progress. Whatever inducements one may originally provide, declining profitability eventually puts an end to pure capital deepening. Further deepening and productivity gains, and hence any further improvement in the growth rate beyond that given by labor force growth, must depend on the pace of technical progress.

But this theoretical result is not nearly as alarming for investment policy as it may at first seem. For some intermediate run, a permanent increase in the portion of output devoted to investment would provide worthwhile gains in the growth rate. More importantly, as the growth rate eventually settled back to its long-run pace, we would still continue to produce at permanently higher *levels* of output; and (unless we overshoot to an inefficiently high investment fraction), we would enjoy permanently higher *levels* of consumption as well. The force of Tobin's analysis is that we are now indeed below our optimal path of consumption; that more investment, although for now at the expense of consumption, would be so productive as to yield preferred, higher consumption paths in the future.

All this raises the question of how much investment would be required for alternative growth goals. It is a difficult question to research because the sources of growth are so interrelated. Each historical dollar of investment has not only added to the stock of physical capital, but has brought with it its own technology. Technical progress, in turn, has entered the production processes of the economy in other ways beside through just the introduction of new capital goods. Finally, the rate of technical progress has no doubt been uneven historically and itself may well be related in a significant way to the level of activity in the economy and how fast it is expanding: The causality between innovation and new investment runs both ways. Granting such uncertainties, Solow suggests investment spending might have to rise from 10 percent to over 12 percent of GNP in order to raise the growth rate over the next decade from 4 percent to 4.25 percent per year. While the output gained by the end of the decade would be considerable—some 2.5 percent of the GNP in the tenth year—this does suggest how large the investment effort must be if faster growth relies entirely on greater tangible investment. Indeed, if we take the required investment to be as great as 12.5 percent of GNP—and Solow admits some would place it well above 12 percent—even after a decade, consumption on the higher path is still not what it would have been had the investment fraction never changed.[1]

Intangible Investment. If the payoff to intangible investment is great enough, growth policies may look considerably more attractive. When account is taken of the historical increases in labor and physical capital used in production, empirical results verify what common sense would suggest: A considerable part of the historical growth of output must be attributed to other factors related to improved quality of the labor and capital used and the efficiency with which they are combined

---

[1] If we take as "consumption" all of the GNP not counted as investment in plant and equipment, it falls from 90 percent to 87.5 percent of GNP as investment rises from 10 percent to 12.5 percent. In this case it takes about twelve years before the consumption level on the 4.25-percent growth path equals that on the 4-percent growth path. If we take 70 percent of GNP as present consumption and consider dropping it to 67.5 percent, the required time before the alternative consumption paths cross is fifteen years.

in production. Ultimately, these must be influenced by the educational attainments of the work force. Thus, education, in addition to possessing its other personal and social values, is an important form of investment. Bowen's paper discusses the economic returns accruing to society from investment in education.

Bowen reviews much of the work that has been done in measuring social rates of return to education and considers many of the problems that beset such measurement. One starting point is the measurement of private rates of return as reflected in the earnings differentials among groups with various amounts of schooling. Some of the difficulties encountered even in this simpler problem include estimating the foregone income of persons in school, the income differentials that are attributable to native ability rather than education, and the nonmonetary benefits of education to those who get positive enjoyment from it apart from any additional income it provides. For college education, Bowen suggests the purely monetary rate of return to education is at least comparable with estimates of the return on plant and equipment expenditures. He argues further that the external, or social, benefits to investment in education, as well as to other human investments, such as better health, far exceed those to investment in physical capital. And, in addition, investments in human capital confer nonmonetary benefits of great importance.

One of the most visible ways in which higher education affects growth is through the activities of research and development. Over the longer run, the supply of research and development effort can be influenced by the educational attainments of the population. But we can influence it over shorter periods as well by investing more of our present resources in these pursuits and by channeling the total research and development effort into its most productive channels.

Nelson notes that present Research and Development is highly concentrated in a few areas. Of the R and D done in industry, over 55 percent is performed by two related industry groups, with three other groups accounting for most of the rest. Is this evidence that deliberate policy steps are needed in this area? The potential gain from innovative efforts varies in different fields; and Jacob Schmookler has assembled impressive verification of his hypothesis that inventive effort is guided by potential profitability.[2] Therefore, one might judge that no deliberate public policy is needed—that effort and resources are being properly guided by market forces—were it not for two facts discussed by Nelson: First, the government creates the market for a great deal of R and D effort, with the Defense Department and National Aeronautics and Space Administration financing some 60 percent of the R and D done by industry at last count. Second, the ability to run the risks of fruitless research and to reap the profits of successful R and D work varies sharply among industries depending, in large part, on their industrial organization. Industrial giants account for a disproportionate share of total research and development for these very good reasons. Yet an appropriate reckoning of social priorities, gains, and risks might well call for a different allocation of effort.

These considerations also suggest why the total R and D effort in the nation probably falls short of the optimum. Society averages the risks of all such undertakings; and society captures the total gain from the successes. Individuals and individual firms cannot do so and therefore stop short of making the optimal effort. And this discrepancy between the social optimal and what the market will provide grows larger the more basic the research involved.

One conclusion that emerges from all this is that growth policy should work on all fronts to be effective. Tangible investment offers the most immediate and certain promise of greater economic growth. Yet, historically, we have gotten a large part of our growth from technical progress rather than mere capital deepening and we know that technical improve-

---

[2] Jacob Schmookler, *Invention and Economic Growth*, Cambridge, Mass.: Harvard University Press, 1966.

ments encourage tangible investment by raising its profitability. On the other hand, while greater emphasis on intangible investment may offer large potential returns, to a great extent its results require embodiment in plant and equipment before they are realized. So far, we simply do not know enough about the interrelations of these effects to sort them out more fully; but that they go very much together seems clear.

GROWTH IN THE LARGER
POLICY FRAMEWORK

It is entirely possible to agree with the arguments that are made here—with Tobin's analysis showing that we want more investment than we are getting, with Lampman's conclusion that our past growth has been justified by increased welfare and that future growth would be accompanied by similar gains, with Cooper's arguments for important national goals —and still have reservations about some future growth policies. For what must be settled is not whether policies for faster growth can serve our whole set of goals well, but which set of policies will in fact serve our composite set of goals best.

In simplest terms, the great attraction of more rapid growth is that it permits us to choose more of everything. The classroom abstraction is that growth enlarges the pie which we are then free to divide up as we please. This same notion lies behind Cooper's description of growth as the great reconciler. But more properly, it should be viewed as the potential reconciler. It may not do to espouse growth policy on the grounds that it will make certain other goals easier to attain without actually providing for their attainment.

Cooper shows that growth in our output can serve our international aims in several ways. And the rapid United States expansion of the past few years has already had some of the effects he describes. Prices of nonferrous base metals, important sources of foreign exchange to many less-developed nations, have risen spectacularly, from a 1961–63 index average of 110 to 153 in 1965. The terms of trade of Latin America as a whole have gone from a 1961–63 index average of 95 to 102 in 1965. These are impressive results, although it must be remembered that they come from an exceptional period of expansion in the United States and are unlikely to be sustained or repeated once expansion slows to the pace of the growth of total capacity here.

But Cooper also argued for faster growth as a means of expanding our direct aid. Yet there has been little connection in recent years between output growth and direct aid to underdeveloped areas. As George Woods, President of the World Bank, recently pointed out,[3] despite a rise of 4 percent to 5 percent annually in the GNP of the industrialized nations, net official aid has remained constant since 1961; on a per capita basis, it has declined by 2 to 3 percent a year.

The failure of the current rapid economic expansion to bring Negro unemployment rates down to tolerable levels is another example. Economists had argued that such expansion was necessary for reducing all unemployment rates, among white as well as non-white workers. It has done so. But in the face of serious structural barriers to employment for Negroes, it has not reduced Negro unemployment far enough, and the disparity between white and non-white economic positions may have grown.

These results are hardly a consequence of growth. But by way of example, they reject any easy connection between growth and all the ultimate goals that growth must serve.

More generally, even if the economists' calculations and society's preferences point to a desire for more rapid growth, for the sacrifice of some present consumption for more later, this conclusion only raises anew many of the most important questions for policy. It must be recognized that rapid growth

[3] Statement of George O. Woods to the Ministerial Meeting of the Development Assistance Committee, O.E.C.D., Paris, July 22, 1965.

leaves a wake of problems along the path of progress. This in itself is no barrier to the pursuit of growth; there is, potentially, a net gain available, problems and all. The reason the problems should concern us is that their incidence is uneven and capricious. They injure some—only a few perhaps—out of all proportion to the gain to them.

A freeway providing efficient transportation between the suburbs and the central city is not always landscaped, to the discomfort of city-dwellers along its route.

A new factory dumping industrial waste into a river is hardly prized by residents too far downstream to benefit from the employment it creates.

A worker displaced by a machine takes little comfort in knowing that this is but another step in the march of technical progress that is raising real wages everywhere else.

This is a small sample; and it is a classic rather than original list. It is chosen in part to emphasize that many of our old problems are aggravated by accelerated growth and change; and in part to show that it is entirely feasible to deal with such problems in a complete growth policy, for important new federal initiatives have recently been taken or proposed dealing with each of these problems—beautification, pollution abatement, and manpower education and training.

What concerns some observers is that such measures already have a woefully lower priority than they deserve. If our national energies can be harnessed to no more than one great economic crusade, they fear the problem areas will continue insufficiently attended if we concentrate now on faster growth. Surely these social critics know that a bigger total level of output could serve their purposes better than a smaller one. They must then be concerned that the outputs in the two cases will differ in more than just size; that in striving hard to enlarge our GNP, we will inevitably alter its composition and change its distribution in directions they dislike.

This may be a valid concern. While some growth-oriented measures also serve other acknowledged social goals, as in the case of improved educational opportunities and medical care, others do not. Many means of enlarging the proportion of business investment in the GNP would also enhance the relative rewards to owners of capital. Whether this should be done is one issue. Whether it could be done without courting inflation in an environment where labor has typically battled to maintain its real share is another. A growth policy, to be really acceptable, must then be complete. It must go below the aggregates to the issues of how its benefits are distributed and how the problems it creates can be minimized and compensated for. And it must make provision for our particular social objectives rather than diverting the national purpose from them. If this is done, the essays in this volume offer considerable evidence in favor of policies for faster growth.

Part II

Measuring the Impact of the 1964 Tax Reduction

BY

Arthur M. Okun

AUTHOR'S NOTE—JUNE 1967[1]

This paper was written during the summer of 1965. It reported on the way the Revenue Act of 1964 had served as a major stimulus to economic activity in the preceding year and a half. Just about the time that this paper was completed, we entered a new chapter in our economic history in which the key fiscal impact on the economy came from the extra defense expenditures required to fulfill our commitments in Southeast Asia. Any analysis of fiscal impact that covered the more recent period could no longer treat monetary policy as a passive supporting force, nor could it continue to ignore the influence of higher levels of aggregate demand on prices. Moreover, an updated version of this paper would revise the quantitative estimates associated with the tax reduction. Both revisions in earlier data and more recent experience would influence the point estimates. But neither the consideration of the most recent period nor the statistical refinement would change the basic conclusion that the tax cut of 1964 carried us a giant step toward full employment.

In the process of doing so, it also had important consequences for economic growth, which justify the inclusion of this topic in a volume of essays dealing with the subject of growth. To be sure, the Revenue Act of 1964 was aimed at the demand, rather than the supply, side of the nation's economy.

[1] This paper was made possible by the able assistance of Allen Lerman.

Its objective and achievement was primarily to put productive capacity to work by raising private demand. Effects on the productive capability of the nation were largely incidental but nonetheless important.

By promoting fuller use of capacity, the tax cut created powerful incentives for growth-oriented activity by business. This was most apparent in the subsequent investment boom with its important widening, deepening, and updating of our capital stock. Fuller employment of labor, meanwhile, encouraged greater efforts in the private training of manpower and improved the mobility and upgrading of our human resources.

Finally, the tax cut set the stage for a heightened interest in public policy to stimulate growth. When the nation was failing to make full use of its existing productive capacity, there were good reasons for policy-makers to be unenthusiastic about measures that promised an accelerated growth of supply capabilities. Indeed, there was even a powerful attraction to proposals that sought deliberately to curtail growth, such as by enforcing artificially a marked shortening of the workweek or earlier retirement of senior workers. The realization of full employment was a prerequisite for the serious consideration of policies to stimulate economic growth. Once we can enjoy an environment of peacetime prosperity, growth policy will come to the fore. And it will owe much to the demonstration through the 1964 Revenue Act that we can make full use of rapidly growing productive capacity.

INTRODUCTION

The best-known fact about the Revenue Act of 1964 is that, in the year and a half since it took effect, economic activity has expanded briskly. But such *post hoc, propter hoc* reasoning will never do. Many things happened early in 1964, and, by reference only to the course of events, one could attribute the buoyant performance of the economy to Illinois' victory in the Rose Bowl or to Goldwater's decision to stand in the New Hampshire primary. *Post hoc, propter hoc* somehow always seems to be on the other guy's side. If the economy had slipped into recession in 1964, it would have been viewed as a refutation of the efficacy of the tax cut. It would have been awfully difficult to get a serious discussion of whether an even worse setback might have occurred if not for the tax cut. At least now one can attract an audience to consider more analytical types of reasoning.

The analytical principles of macro-economics argue that rises in the incomes of individuals stimulate their consumer spending, while some combination of profit rates, cash flow, and sales is important as a determinant of business investment. The Revenue Act of 1964 affected these variables directly by adding to personal disposable income and to corporate profits after taxes. To the extent that the tax cut raised spending by consumers and businessmen through this direct route, it should also be credited with additional effects through the familiar multiplier process, whereby the spending of one individual or firm adds to the incomes and hence to the spending of others.

In the area of consumer spending, just a casual observation of the recent aggregative data suggests that there must be some validity to this story. By the second quarter of 1965, consumption expenditures had registered a remarkable rise of $45 billion from their rate in the last quarter of 1963—the quarter immediately preceding the tax cut. Such an increase over six quarters is unmatched in our peacetime history. If one ignores the tax cut, that surge is an insoluble mystery. On the other hand, the expansion of consumer purchases is easily accounted for by the income gains associated with the tax cut and the hypothesis that consumers have treated the increase in take-home pay from the tax reduction in the same way they treat increases in take-home pay from other sources.

By definition, individuals do something with income gains

—they cannot ignore them and, according to the principles of utility maximization, they will not throw income away. Hence, the issue is how they allocate the proceeds between consumption and saving.[2] Both on the average and on the margin, the bulk of disposable income is consumed. If tax-cut gains are treated like other increases in income, most will be consumed and only a little will be added to saving.

The premise that tax-cut dollars are treated like other dollars of additional income is the foundation of the analysis. It is only fair to give warning that once this premise is accepted, the rest of the story follows readily. For our historical time-series data yield consumption-income relationships in which the marginal propensity to consume is very close to the average. Similarly, the quantitative record on investment tells us statistically that profits and sales have substantial effects on capital outlays. Indeed, this fundamental premise is the reason that so many economists expected so much from the 1964 Revenue Act. This premise can be subjected to some empirical check, although it cannot be supported by any refined verification from aggregative time-series data. If relationships established in the past hold up reasonably well after the tax cut, when tax-cut gains are added to other dollars of income, that supports the premise. But the real appeal is analytical: It is hard to see why people should want to segregate tax-cut dollars and treat them or think of them differently from other gains in their pay-checks or their corporate tills.

Given the fundamental premise, the analysis of the effects of the tax cut is an exercise in the dynamics of income-expenditure relationships. But that does not mean it is a simple exercise. Virtually every issue in aggregative eco-

---

[2] The Department of Commerce's recently amended conceptual framework introduces a new third option for consumers. They are now free to engage in personal transfers to businesses or to foreigners by paying interest on personal debt or making gifts to persons overseas. All empirical work in this paper is based on the revised national accounts data shown in the *Survey of Current Business*, August 1965.

nometrics bears on the result. The answer ought to be based ⌐
on a fully articulated set of economic relationships that takes
proper account of all the ways that everything depends on
everything else in the economy. You will not be surprised to ⌐
learn that the estimates developed below do not rest on such
a complete analysis of the economy. Instead, they depend on
a few key estimated functions and a liberal sprinkling of assumptions (which I note along the way) that other possible
effects can be ignored.

In fact, I will temporarily assume that the only effects that
need to be considered are those on consumption and personal
disposable income. This gives us the familiar case of the pure
consumption multiplier, where any and all effects on investment are ignored, and where the increment in Gross National
Product is taken to consist entirely of consumption. The consumption gain can be divided into two parts. One reflects the
direct result of tax reduction in raising personal disposable
income, and the second stems from the extra incomes generated
by additions to consumer spending. The first of these is logi-
cally prior to the second. Nevertheless, because consumers do
not adjust spending fully and immediately to the increases in
their incomes, the two parts will overlap chronologically, and
both will contribute to the growing increment in GNP over
time.

The pure consumption case is interesting and instructive,
and its dynamics are challenging. But it is certainly misleading.
Nobody can really believe that a surge in consumer spending
and a major rise in corporate profits and sales would have no
impact on outlays for plant, equipment, and additional inventory. We must move on into the world of the accelerator
or supermultiplier, as difficult as it is to quantify that world.
Hence, I will emphasize quantitative estimates of the effects
of tax reduction when both consumption and investment outlays are taken into account. But first I must back up and start
at the beginning.

THE SIZE OF THE TAX CUT

The first question in evaluating the impact of the 1964 tax cut is how big was it? And the answer is not as easy as one would wish. We can estimate that the tax reduction for individuals lowered liabilities on Federal individual income taxes by $6.7 billion for 1964 and by $11.5 billion for 1965. But the reduced liability is not the way the tax cut shows up in personal disposable income.

Our national income accounting takes the view that the spending of individuals (unlike that of corporations) is influenced by income taxes when these are paid rather than when the liabilities accrue. Actual payments were affected when the withholding rate declined from 18 percent to 14 percent in March 1964. The corresponding reduction in withheld taxes during 1964 amounted to a good deal more than $6.7 billion; indeed, it was above $8 billion. During the year, people were getting increases in take-home pay that exceeded the reductions in their tax liabilities. In part, this was associated with a reduced claim on the Federal Government for tax refunds early in 1965—any nontaxable dollar to which withholding had been applied generated a fourteen-cent refund rather than the eighteen-cent refund associated with the old withholding rate. Moreover, it was no secret that the 14 percent rate applied to ten months of the year would leave many people on less of a pay-as-you-go basis than they had been under the previous regime. In principle, anyone who changed his withholding voluntarily to maintain his degree of "pay-as-you-go" should have this adjustment subtracted from the dollar value of the tax cut for 1964.

There obviously were some such adjustments of withholding on a voluntary basis. Quantitatively, however, the best guess today is that they did not amount to much. Similarly, some of the self-employed reduced their estimated tax payments in June and September of 1964 in light of the lower tax rates. But, again, the adjustment does not seem to have been quantitatively significant and it would have operated in the other direction. Hence, we get a good approximation to the effect of the tax cut on disposable income through 1964 if we take actual withheld taxes after March, collected at a 14 percent rate, and apply a $2/7$ ratio to them, so as to allow for the decline of four percentage points. For the first half of 1965, we must allow for the reduced refunds and the somewhat larger "clean-up payments" on the 1964 liabilities, which reduce the magnitude of the tax cut.

In principle, we should calculate the dollar value of the tax cut by applying the lower rates to incomes as they would have been in the absence of the tax cut and not to incomes as they actually turned out. But this difference is minor, and there are enough big problems to justify compromises on the little ones. I have rounded down the dollar estimates to make a rough allowance for this difference. The resulting estimates in billions of dollars (seasonally adjusted at annual rates) run as follows:

1964-I	3.2
-II	10.0
-III	10.0
-IV	10.0
1965-I	9.0
-II	9.5
-III	10.0
-IV	10.0

For corporations, the calculation is easier, simply because we treat taxes on a liability basis. The two-point reduction in the corporate tax rate for 1964, augmented by a switch between normal and surtax rates and by a liberalization of the investment credit, added up to $1.8 billion for the year. Another rate cut of two points took effect in 1965, and brought the 1965 total to $3 billion. The really important question about the corporate tax cut is whether it was shifted (either forward to consumers or backward to workers) or whether its benefits remained in the corporate sector. Without great conviction, I assume that there was no shifting in the short-run period covered by this paper.

THE PURE CONSUMPTION MULTIPLIER

The case of the pure consumption multiplier assumes away many of the difficult issues. To deal with it, all we need to know is (a) how much the tax cut adds directly to disposable income, (b) how much each dollar increase in disposable income adds to consumption, and (c) how much a dollar of additional consumption, in turn, adds further to disposable income.

The basic ingredient is the consumption-disposable income relationship. This is the most famous of all quantitative economic relationships, and it has appeared in all shapes, sizes, degrees of disaggregation, and other variations on the Keynesian theme. I shall use a simple form which treats consumer spending as a single total. It makes aggregate consumption in the current quarter depend only on aggregate consumption of the preceding quarter and on the personal disposable income of the current quarter. The presence of lagged consumption does, however, introduce a cumulative influence of the whole history of consumption and income on current consumption. The lagged consumption variable implies the presence of habit persistence or inertia in living standards. The equation has a respectable genealogy, going back (at least) to an article by T. M. Brown in *Econometrica* of July 1952.

The equation is spelled out in Table 1, as are its implications. According to it, an additional dollar of disposable income in the current quarter raises current consumption by 37.1 cents. If the income gain is maintained, consumption in the next period will be above its base level by 59.7 cents— the sum of 37.1 cents and .609 of 37.1 cents. Ultimately, the

TABLE 1

Incremental Consumption Associated with
a Maintained $1 Increase in Disposable Income

Quarter	Incremental Consumption
0	0
1	.371
2	.597
3	.735
4	.819
5	.870
6	.901
.	.
.	.
.	.
∞	.949

$$C_t = -1.40 + .371 \ Y_t + .609 \ C_{t-1}$$
(billions of current dollars; fitted to
period from 1954-I to 1964-IV)*
$$\bar{R}^2 = .999 \qquad \bar{S}_E = 1.71$$

* A homogeneous form $C_t/Y_t = .343 + .635 \ C_{t-1}/Y_t$ gives virtually identical results.

effect on consumption reaches 94.9 cents, as can be seen by solving the equation for $C_t = C_{t-1}$.

The intercept of this equation is a small negative number, surprisingly suggesting that the marginal propensity to consume is larger than the average propensity. But the difference is very small and has no economic significance despite the statistical significance of the intercept. If the consumption function is forced through the origin and fitted homogeneously, one obtains a very similar equation which yields essentially the same results over time. These equations were also fitted with lagged income as well as lagged consumption, but the results were not improved. Asset variables deserve an opportunity to help explain consumption, but they did not get their chance in this analysis. Nor was there any attempt to disaggregate consumption, such as by separating out expenditures for durable goods.

TABLE 2

Marginal Shares of Receipts
from a Maintained $1 Increase in Gross National Product

					Quarter	
		0	1	2	3 ⋯ 6	
1.	*Gross National Product*	0	1.000	1.000	1.000	1.000
2.	Corporate Profits before Taxes	0	.667	.340	.340	.340
3.	Corporate Taxes	0	.264	.134	.134	.134
3a.	Federal	0	.248	.127	.127	.127
3b.	State and Local	0	.015	.008	.008	.008
4.	Corporate Profits after Taxes	0	.404	.206	.206	.206
5.	Corporate Dividend Payments	0	.020	.029	.037	.058
6.	Undistributed Corporate Profits	0	.384	.177	.169	.148
7.	Indirect Business Taxes	0	.056	.056	.056	.056
7a.	Federal	0	.023	.023	.023	.023
7b.	State and Local	0	.033	.033	.033	.033
8.	Social Insurance Taxes	0	.011	.025	.025	.026
8a.	Federal	0	.009	.021	.021	.022
8b.	State and Local	0	.002	.004	.004	.004
9.	Transfer Payments	0	−.035	−.035	−.035	−.035
9a.	Federal	0	−.035	−.035	−.035	−.035
9b.	State and Local	0	0	0	0	0
10.	*Personal Income*	0	.251	.572	.580	.600
11.	Personal Taxes	0	.036	.082	.083	.086
11a.	Federal	0	.030	.068	.068	.071
11b.	State and Local	0	.006	.015	.015	.015
12.	*Disposable Personal Income*	0	.215	.490	.497	.514
	Addendum: Net Government					
	Receipts	0	.402	.333	.334	.338
	Federal	0	.345	.273	.274	.277
	State and Local	0	.057	.060	.060	.061

Details may not add to totals due to rounding.

$(10) = (1) - (3) - (6) - (7) - (8) + (9)$
$(12) = (10) - (11)$

Corporate profits were estimated marginally from:

$$(P + CCA)_t = -6.4229 + .1686\ Y_t + .3267\ \Delta Y_t - .5502\ X_t$$
$$\bar{R}^2 = .961 \qquad \bar{S}_E = 1.403 \qquad \text{d.w.} = .846$$

where $(P + CCA)$ is Corporate Profits before Taxes including Inventory Valuation Adjustment plus Corporate Capital Consumption Allowances
Y is Gross National Product
and X is a measure of excess capacity associated with unemployment.
$(U - .0400) \times$ GNP, where U is the unemployment rate.

The equation was fitted to quarterly data (seasonally adjusted at annual rates) for the period 1954-I to 1964-IV, and variables were measured in billions of current dollars.

The incremental calculation estimates that the unemployment rate is reduced by one percentage point by a 3.2 percent increment in GNP.

Throughout, capital consumption allowances are taken to be unaffected by changes in GNP.

Dividend payments were determined quarterly on the margin from:

$$D_t = .92 \, D_{t-1} + .05 \, AP_t$$

where AP is Corporate Profits after Taxes.

Corporate profits taxes were estimated at 39.5 percent of corporate profits.

Other taxes were estimated by taking the actual 1964 ratio to either GNP (Y) or Personal Income (Y_p), as appropriate, and using the following elasticities:

Federal Indirect Taxes	0.9	on Y
State and Local Indirect Taxes	0.5	on Y
Federal Social Insurance Taxes	0.75	on Y_p
State and Local Insurance Taxes	0.75	on Y_p
Federal Personal Taxes	1.2	on Y_p
State and Local Personal Taxes	1.2	on Y_p

The consumption function alone would enable us to estimate the consumption gains associated with the direct income gains of the tax cut. But those direct income gains do not account for the full increase in personal disposable income. Part of the gain in disposable income results from the addition to consumption. Hence, we need to know how much each extra dollar of consumption (or, equivalently, of GNP) adds to disposable income. The best way I know to deal with the marginal share of disposable income in GNP is to subtract the other leakages that do not go into disposable income. It turns out that the marginal share of disposable income in GNP is considerably less than the average ratio of disposable income to GNP. One major reason for this is that, in the short run, when GNP increases, Government transfer payments do not keep pace; in fact they are actually reduced through a decline in unemployment insurance benefits. The other and even more important reason is that corporate profits get a very large marginal share of GNP, particularly when the increase is sudden. Since dividends adjust very slowly through time, the bulk of the marginal share of profits is a withdrawal from disposable income.

[3] I have discussed this elsewhere. See "Short-Term Forecasting by the President's Council of Economic Advisers" in O.E.C.D., *Techniques of Economic Forecasting*, Paris, 1965, pp. 163–65.

As noted in Table 2, I have explained the sum of profits and corporate capital consumption allowances, using as independent variables the level of GNP, the change in GNP from the preceding quarter, and a utilization variable which multiplies GNP by the excess of the unemployment rate over 4 percent. On the basis of this equation, the marginal corporate share is a strikingly large 67 percent when GNP rises in a quarter, and it remains at 34 percent in succeeding quarters if the gain in GNP is maintained. The importance of fixed costs supplies good analytical reasons for a large marginal corporate share. Still, the quantitative estimates of the marginal share derived from equations are always surprisingly large to me. After investigating the effect of alternative variables on the magnitude of the corporate marginal share, I bow to the persistence of the empirical results.

The other leakages in Table 2 are based on elasticity estimates which have a variety of underpinnings. They are nowhere nearly so troublesome as profits in the probable error they introduce in the marginal disposable income calculation. Taking account of the various leakages, we conclude that a dollar increase in GNP raises disposable income in the current quarter by 21.5 cents; if the GNP gain is maintained, the disposable income gain reaches about 50 cents in the second quarter. It keeps creeping up slightly because dividends keep rising very gradually in response to the increase in corporate profits. The whole process can be simplified and summarized adequately by assuming that, in the second and succeeding quarters, the marginal share of disposable income in GNP levels off at .505. In the pure consumption case, there is one further influence to take into account: The corporate tax reduction generates extra dividends through time. Quantitatively, this does not amount to much; but it is registered in the results shown in Table 3.

Now we have, in effect, a two-equation system. The marginal consumption tells us how much added consumption is generated by extra disposable incomes; while the marginal

TABLE 3

Sources of Gains in Disposable Income
(Pure Consumption Multiplier)

(in billions of current dollars)

	1964				1965	
	I	II	III	IV	I	II
Direct gain from personal tax reduction	3.2	10.0	10.0	10.0	9.0	9.5
Dividends attributable to corporate tax reduction	0.1	0.2	0.3	0.3	0.4	0.6
Induced gains:						
a) Due to GNP gain of preceding quarter	—	0.8	2.6	4.1	5.3	6.0
b) Due to additional GNP gain in current quarter	0.3	0.7	0.6	0.5	0.3	0.3
Total increment in personal disposable income	3.6	11.7	13.5	14.9	15.1	16.4

Details may not add to total because of rounding.

The results of Table 2 are used here in a simplified form, which assumes that the marginal share of disposable income is constant at .505 after a lag of one quarter. The simultaneous share is taken at .215 as shown in Table 2. Accordingly, the *induced* gain in disposable income consists of:

a) .505 of the preceding quarter's gain for GNP plus
b) .215 of the *increase* in the GNP gain in the current quarter.

The induced gains in disposable income shown here are calculated from the bottom line of Table 4. "Gain" or "increment" for a given quarter refers to the amount over and above the hypothetical no-tax-cut situation; it does not denote the quarter-to-quarter change.

disposable income-GNP relationship tells us what further gains in disposal income are produced by added consumption. Tables 3 and 4 show the numerical solutions of this system. By the fourth quarter of 1964, through the pure consumption route, disposable income is estimated to have been $15.1 billion higher as a result of the tax cut and consumption to have been $10.5 billion higher. These gains continue to expand in the first half of 1965 but at a slower rate. In part, the leveling off reflects the downward bump in the size of the

TABLE 4

Consumption and GNP Gains Related to Disposable Income Gains
(Pure Consumption Multiplier)

Quarter	Gain in disposable income	Resulting gain in consumption in:					
		1964-I	1964-II	1964-III	1964-IV	1965-I	1965-II
1964:							
I	3.6	1.3	0.8	0.5	0.3	0.2	0.1
II	11.7		4.3	2.6	1.6	1.0	0.6
III	13.5			5.0	3.0	1.9	1.1
IV	14.9				5.6	3.4	2.1
1965:							
I	15.1					5.6	3.4
II	16.4						6.1
Total consumption (or GNP) gain in given quarter		1.3	5.1	8.1	10.5	12.0	13.4

Details may not add to totals because of rounding.

The cells above show the "phasing-out" of income gains into consumption gains in accordance with the consumption equation set forth in Table 1. That consumption equation and the disposable income relationship summarized in the note to Table 3 form a two-equation system in consumption and disposable income.

In the "pure consumption multiplier" case, the GNP gain is set equal to the consumption gain.

tax cut for the first half of 1965; in part, it suggests that the process was, by that time, beginning to approach its full effect.

But the ultimate full effect is considerably larger than the $13.4 billion gain in consumption shown for the second quarter of 1965. Holding the personal tax cut at $10 billion and the corporate reduction at $3 billion, we would ultimately reach a consumption gain of more than $21.2 billion.

The corporate tax reduction would be credited with a $3 billion contribution to consumption after the very long wait required for dividends to be fully adjusted. This is not a great performance as a consumption stimulus, but corporate tax cuts have never been expected to star in that respect.

The bulk of the ultimate consumption gain—$18.2 billion —would be attributable to the personal tax reduction. Based on a .949 marginal propensity to consume and a .505 marginal share of disposable income, the steady-state multiplier is 1.82. Given the nature of this calculation, "close to two" remains a good familiar approximation to the pure consumption multiplier for a tax cut.

INDUCED INVESTMENT

Now I move to the more difficult but more realistic situation in which induced investment is recognized. We will continue to assume that neither net exports nor residential construction is affected by the tax cut or by the subsequent increases in incomes. These simplifying assumptions are not likely to be quantitatively important and at least they are offsetting in direction: Net exports would be lowered by higher GNP, while residential construction would be favorably affected, given the state of credit conditions. The induced effects we deal with are those on business fixed investment and inventory investment.

The choice of an equation for explaining business fixed investment is exceedingly difficult. Here, we cannot take advantage of the survey data and other barometric indicators that are so helpful in forecasting plant and equipment. Sales, utilization measures, and cash flow variables all have excellent claims for appearing in the equation. But when all of these are allowed to compete in equations fitted from time-series data, chaos results. The coefficients are highly unstable with respect to the choice of lags and the specification of variables. I trust that the econometric conflict between cash flow and accelerator models will be settled some day, but I am convinced that the decisive battle will not be fought with aggregative time-series data.

Many time-series equations with a few lags and a few variables perform about equally well. A cash flow equation with four quarterly lags in that single variable gave good results and reasonable coefficients. That is what I am using, as shown in Table 5. To the extent that cash flow really serves here as a proxy for other influences, such as sales and utilization, this should not be disturbing. The reliance on cash flow does credit the corporate tax cut with direct influence, but the omission of after-tax profits in the investment equation would assume that it had no direct effect. According to this equation, a dollar of extra after-tax corporate profits ultimately raises investment by seventy-five cents, working out its effects over the succeeding four quarters, as shown in Table 5.

The results of the inventory equation are also shown in Table 5. Inventory investment is explained using lagged stocks, lagged inventory investment, and current and last quarter's final sales of GNP. This equation and other inventory equations was a terrible estimator for the period from the second quarter of 1959 to the first quarter of 1960, when inventory investment was dominated by first the expectation, then the realization, and finally the recovery from the steel strike. Nevertheless, other periods of steel-dominated inventory activity did not show unreasonable results. Hence, the four misbehaving quarters were thrown out of the sample from which the equation was calculated. Because of the presence of the stock variable, there is no ultimate maintained level of inventory investment. As Table 5 shows, the induced inventory investment associated with a $1 maintained increase in GNP begins to decline after three quarters. It would eventually turn negative and oscillate, ultimately converging to zero.

The fixed investment and inventory equations do not include any monetary variables. In principle, they belong here. I would certainly expect a significant change in the costs or availability of credit to have an important influence on business investment. In practice, dealing with the period from early 1964 through mid-1965, I cannot believe that the omission of monetary variables can make a serious difference. By any measure of interest rates or credit conditions I know,

TABLE 5

*Increments in Business Fixed and Inventory Investment
from a Maintained $1 Increase in Final Sales of GNP*

Quarter	Business fixed investment	Inventory investment
0	0	0
1	0	.041
2	.118	.163
3	.134	.207
4	.163	.197
5	.176	.157
6	.154	.105

Business fixed investment was calculated marginally from:

$$I_t = 9.02 + .293 F_{t-1} + .182 F_{t-2} + .162 F_{t-3} + .110 F_{t-4}$$
$$R^2 = .968 \qquad \bar{S}_E = 1.30 \qquad d.w. = .609$$

F is corporate cash flow (corporate profits after tax, including inventory valuation adjustment, plus corporate capital consumption allowances).

The equation is fitted to quarterly data for 1954-I through 1964-IV and all variables are quarterly totals at seasonally adjusted annual rates expressed in billions of current dollars.

F was estimated marginally using the profits function set forth in Table 2 and an estimated profits tax share of 39.5 percent, as noted in Table 2.

Inventory investment was calculated from:

$$V_t = -45.56 - .1715 H_{t-1} + .5842 V_{t-1} + .0428 S_t + .1099 S_{t-1}$$
$$R^2 = .733 \qquad \bar{S}_E = 1.908 \qquad d.w. = 1.886$$

where V is the change in Business Inventories;
   H is V cumulated from 1947-I;
and S is GNP Final Sales.

Variables are quarterly totals, seasonally adjusted at annual rates in billions of 1958 dollars. The equation was fitted to 1954-I to 1964-IV but omitting the period from 1959-II to 1960-I.

there were no significant monetary changes that would have either stimulated or restrained investment to a major degree. Obviously, the rising incomes and investment of this period generated increased demands for financial assets and for loans. In this environment, the maintenance of stable interest rates and stable credit conditions required action by the monetary authorities to expand the reserve base more rapidly so as to accommodate expansion.

In this sense, monetary policies made a major contribution

to the advance, but that contribution can be appropriately viewed as permissive rather than causal. The monetary authorities supplied a good sound set of tires for the economy to roll on, but they did not contribute the engine. That came from fiscal policies. If monetary policy had been the driving force, that would have shown up—at least initially—in a decline of interest rates and a relaxation of credit conditions.

It is reasonable to ask how much slower the overall economic advance might have been and how much less expansionary the tax cut would have been if monetary policy had not been accommodating. One could hypothesize an alternative monetary policy which held down the growth of bank reserves or the money supply (or other liquidity variables) to some stated degree. And one could then try to assess what difference this tighter monetary policy would have made in the pace of economic advance. That would be an interesting statistical exercise. It just does not happen to be the particular statistical exercise which this paper attempts to perform.

We can now put the whole process in motion, using the inventory and the investment equations along with the disposable income relationship and the consumption function discussed earlier. The results are shown in Table 6. The gains in GNP are, of course, larger than those estimated in the pure consumption case. Indeed, consumption itself rises more strongly because of the greater induced gains in disposable income. And, after a slow start, the investment components are contributing about one-third of the estimated total gain in GNP after the fourth quarter of 1964. The total gain in GNP reaches $17.1 billion in the final quarter of 1964 and goes on to $24.4 billion in the second quarter of 1965. If we continue the process for another two quarters, the GNP increase would exceed $30 billion in the fourth quarter of 1965.

And it will be rising. With a $10 billion personal tax cut and a $3 billion corporate reduction, the GNP gain would ultimately be $36.2 billion, $7.8 billion in business fixed in-

TABLE 6

GNP Gains by Components Allowing for Induced Investment
(in billions of current dollars)

	1964				1965	
	I	II	III	IV	I	II
Gains in:						
Corporate Cash Flow	2.4	4.1	5.2	6.1	8.0	8.8
Direct from profits tax reduction	1.8	1.8	1.8	1.8	3.0	3.0
Induced profits before tax	1.0	3.8	5.6	7.2	8.3	9.6
Less: Induced profits taxes	−0.4	−1.5	−2.2	−2.8	−3.3	−3.8
Disposable Income	3.6	11.9	14.5	17.1	18.5	21.2
Direct from personal tax reduction	3.2	10.0	10.0	10.0	9.0	9.5
Dividends attributed to corporate tax reduction	0.1	0.1	0.2	0.3	0.4	0.5
Induced	0.3	1.8	4.2	6.8	9.1	11.2
Consumption	1.3	5.2	8.6	11.6	13.9	16.3
Business Fixed Investment	—	0.7	1.6	2.6	3.7	4.8
Inventory Investment	0.1	0.4	1.2	2.1	2.8	3.2
Total GNP	1.4	6.3	11.4	16.3	20.5	24.4

vestment and $28.4 billion in consumption. In this final situation, inventory investment would no longer contribute to the gain.

Of this "final" $36.2 billion gain in GNP, $25.9 billion results from the personal tax reduction and $10.3 billion from the corporate tax cut. The "steady state" multiplier for personal taxes is 2.59. The ultimate multiplier for the corporate tax cut is estimated at 3.4. But the corporate cut takes a much longer time to approach its full effects, because dividends creep up so slowly and gradually. Throughout the first two years following a tax cut, the estimated impact per dollar of the personal tax reduction is substantially greater than that of the cut for corporations. Moreover, we should recognize the possibility that the cash flow character of the investment equation may be too generous to the corporate tax cut.

According to these results, the Federal Government received $7 billion of extra net receipts in the second quarter of 1965 (on a national income accounts basis) as a result of the gains attributable to the tax cut. By this Federal budgetary criterion, the tax cut had paid for more than half of itself by then, and the fraction was rising. In addition, state and local governments were the beneficiaries of an estimated $1.5 billion increase in net receipts in the second quarter. In the ultimate situation, the induced gain in Federal net receipts would be $10 billion, and the state and local gain $2.2 billion, adding to a total that nearly matches the $13 billion of tax reduction.

CONCLUSION

This is not the first quantitative estimate that has been made for the Revenue Act of 1964; and it will not be the last. I trust also that it will not be the best. At the Council of Economic Advisers, we hope to improve the tools needed in this analysis and to remedy some of the limitations I have noted above.

Nevertheless, the results shown in Table 6 looks sensible and plausible to me. One way of viewing the conclusions is to consider what they imply about the hypothetical world in which no tax reduction had taken place. The hypothetical no-tax-cut world is constructed by subtracting from actual national accounts variables the estimated gains from the tax cut over the six quarters from the beginning of 1964 to mid-1965. Instead of a rapid growth in GNP of more than $10 billion a quarter in that period, the world without a tax cut has an average quarterly increase of $6.3 billion, as shown in the accompanying chart. When the same thing is done for the other key variables, the results form a consistent pattern —slow growth in disposable income, small advances in consumption, and a leveling off in fixed investment in the first half of 1965 following some slippage in corporate profits during 1964. This no-tax-cut world would have shown rising unemployment and sagging operating rates.

I suggested at the outset one possible check on the fundamental premise that tax cut dollars are treated like other dollars: It consists of looking at empirical relationships established in the past to see whether they went haywire in the period following the tax cut. I can report that the equations held up quite well. Of course, they do not fit perfectly during the last year and a half, but neither did they fit perfectly in the years prior to the tax cut.

In the consumption function, there were sizable errors for two quarters, a $4.5 billion overestimate in the fourth quarter of 1964 and an offsetting $3.5 billion underestimate in the first quarter of 1965. In view of the slow deliveries of new cars during the auto strikes of the autumn of 1964 and the subsequent extraordinary catch-up, this pattern seems perfectly sensible. The profits equation fits unusually well during 1964 and the first half of 1965. Its largest error is in the second quarter of 1965, when it understates the level of profits by $1.7 billion; during the sample period, its standard error of estimate was $1.4 billion. The root-mean-square error in the inventory equation for the six quarters was identical to its $1.9 billion standard error of estimate over the sample period. Fixed investment is exceedingly well estimated for the first half of 1964; but it is underestimated consistently thereafter by amounts ranging from $1.2 to $3.5 billion and averaging $2 billion per quarter. There are grounds for suspicion that the investment equation we have used may have been conservative in its estimate of the induced effects stemming from personal tax reduction.

According to the estimates cited above, the tax cuts of 1964 are credited with a $25 billion contribution to our GNP by mid-1965, a $30 billion effect by the end of 1965, and an ultimate $36 billion increment. I have mentioned many reasons

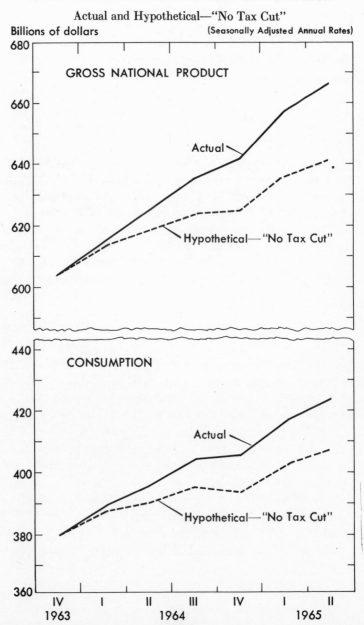

GROSS NATIONAL PRODUCT AND CONSUMPTION

Actual and Hypothetical—"No Tax Cut"

Billions of dollars   (Seasonally Adjusted Annual Rates)

GROSS NATIONAL PRODUCT

Actual

Hypothetical— "No Tax Cut"

CONSUMPTION

Actual

Hypothetical— "No Tax Cut"

IV   I   II   III   IV   I   II
1963   1964   1965

why these point estimates should be viewed as the center of a sizable range. Even with all the appropriate qualifications, these results provide important analytical confirmation that the Revenue Act of 1964 lived up to the intentions and expectations of its advocates, and that it has delivered a powerful stimulus to economic expansion.

Part III

Monetary and Fiscal Policies for Economic Growth

BY

Warren L. Smith

INTRODUCTION

In a modern, predominantly free-enterprise nation such as the United States, the central government must accept responsibility for the stability of the economy—that is, for the prevention of excessive unemployment on the one hand and excessive price inflation on the other. There is agreement on this matter not only among political liberals but among most conservatives as well, although, of course, there are still differences of opinion as to the extent of the responsibility, the precise methods to be employed to fulfill it, and, in particular, the selection of the appropriate balance between the goals of price stability and high employment in given circumstances. Still, the area of agreement is far more important than the specific points of disagreement. Indeed, the responsibility of the Federal Government in this regard has been recognized by both major political parties and was formalized in the Employment Act of 1946.[1]

The maintenance of economic stability is primarily a matter of regulating aggregate demand for goods and services. The accepted instruments for controlling demand are primarily

---

[1] The intellectual foundation for this view of governmental responsibility was laid in the 1930's by Lord Keynes when he demonstrated that while the free market is an institution of great social utility in organizing production and allocating resources in an efficient manner without detailed central planning, the modern free-enterprise economy does not contain adequate built-in mechanisms for maintaining overall economic stability. See J. M. Keynes, *The General Theory of Employment, Interest, and Money*, New York: Harcourt, Brace and Co., 1936.

the monetary policies of the Federal Reserve System, which exert their influence by altering the supply of money and the cost and availability of credit, and the fiscal policies of the Federal Government, which affect the aggregate flow of purchasing power and spending by altering the relation between Federal tax collections and expenditures.[2]

In the last few years, an additional dimension has been added to the discussion and analysis of economic stabilization: It has come to be recognized that the capacity of the economy to produce goods and services grows month by month and year by year. Full employment and reasonable price stability can be maintained only if aggregate demand grows in pace with productive capacity. We no longer feel, as we used to, that we can indulge in self-congratulation merely because the national income in the current year exceeds that of the previous year, thereby "breaking all records." We now recognize that income and product need to expand each year by as much as the growth of productive capacity if we are to maintain a healthy economy and avoid rising unemployment. On the other hand, if we permit aggregate demand to expand more rapidly than productive capacity, inflationary pressures will result. That is, we must run hard—but not too hard—merely to avoid falling behind.

Thus, recognition that monetary and fiscal policies to maintain full employment and stable prices must be formulated in a framework which makes allowance for the growth of productive capacity is now reasonably well established. Beyond this, it is now accepted by many economists, both in and out

---

[2] Even in the 1920's, of course, the Federal Reserve System, established in 1914 to correct structural defects in the banking system which had led to repeated and sometimes disastrous banking crises in the late nineteenth and early twentieth centuries, came to accept some responsibility for regulating the supply of money and credit in the interest of economic stabilization. Then, in the 1940's and 1950's, a number of economists, following up the work of Lord Keynes, developed the economic theory underlying fiscal policy—that is, the deliberate use of the Federal budget as an instrument of overall economic regulation.

of the Federal Government, that by skillful use of monetary and fiscal policies we may be able not only to keep aggregate demand growing in pace with capacity but also to influence the growth of capacity itself.

FULL EMPLOYMENT AND ECONOMIC GROWTH

For purposes of our discussion, the productive capacity of the economy is the output of goods and services that can be produced under conditions of full employment. However, full employment is not an easy concept to define satisfactorily. It can scarcely mean the complete absence of unemployment, since, under almost any conceivable circumstances, there will be a certain amount of so-called "frictional unemployment," resulting from the fact that some workers are always in the process of moving from one job to another.

The best way to arrive at a workable definition of full employment is in terms of the behavior of the price level. Beyond some point, further reduction of unemployment through an expansion of demand will lead to progressively stronger inflationary tendencies for three reasons. First, as production expands, plant capacity bottlenecks are likely to develop in some industries, leading to a rise in the prices of the products of these industries while there is still excess plant capacity available in other parts of the economy. Second, shortages of certain types of labor may be encountered, leading to sharply rising wages which push up prices at a time when the general level of employment is still substantial. Third, as expansion of demand reduces the general level of unemployment and at the same time leads to rising business sales and profits, the strategic position of labor unions in collective bargaining negotiations becomes stronger relative to that of employers, causing wages to rise more rapidly than labor productivity is

increasing, thereby raising labor costs and pushing up prices.[3]
Full employment may be defined as the lowest level of unemployment that can be achieved without encountering significant inflationary pressures—or, somewhat more generally,
as that level of unemployment beyond which, in the opinion
of the responsible public officials (whose decisions presumably
reflect the views of the general public), the social benefits of
a further reduction in unemployment are not worth the social
costs of the inflation associated therewith.

The Kennedy Administration selected a 4 percent unemployment rate as its tentative definition of full employment—
its so-called "interim" unemployment target—in 1961. That
is, the Administration presumably believed that it would be
possible to reduce unemployment to 4 percent of the labor
force without encountering a serious problem of inflation.[4]
Although one might quarrel with the selection of this particular percentage as a definition of full employment, the specific
definition is not important for our present purposes, and I
shall accordingly accept it as a working assumption.

[3] The first two conditions referred to—plant capacity bottlenecks
and shortages of certain types of labor—can presumably be corrected
by a once-and-for-all adjustment of prices which would adapt patterns
of demand and supply to coincide with available resources. Since prices
are, in general, more flexible upward than downward, this price adjustment would probably require some rise in the general level of prices.
Strictly speaking, such a "one-shot" upward price adjustment does not
constitute inflation, since inflation means a *continuing* rise in the price
level. In practice, however, the distinction is a difficult one to apply,
especially because the "one-shot" adjustment would take some time to
work its way through the price structure and while this process was
going on would be practically indistinguishable from "genuine" inflation.

[4] During the current expansion, which began in the first quarter of
1961, wholesale prices did not rise appreciably during the first four
years while the unemployment rate was falling from 6.8 percent to 4.8
percent. Beginning early in 1965, however, prices began to rise rather
sharply; from the first quarter of 1965 to the first quarter of 1966, wholesale prices rose by 4.2 percent as the unemployment rate declined quite
rapidly to 3.8 percent. However, during the ensuing year, price pressures
moderated considerably while the unemployment rate held steady at
just under 4 percent.

On this basis, we may regard the Gross National Product (GNP) that can be produced when unemployment is 4 percent as a measure of the aggregate productive capacity of the economy. The smooth curve in Figure 1 depicts, at least crudely, the growth of productive capacity in this sense. Capacity GNP, represented by the smooth curve in Figure 1, is valued at 1966 prices, and the assumption is that it was equal to actual GNP in mid-1955 when the unemployment rate was approximately 4 percent. The growth rate of capacity GNP is assumed to be 3.5 percent from mid-1955 to the end of 1962, 3.75 percent from then until the end of 1965, and 4 percent thereafter.[5] The broken line in Figure 1 traces the movement of actual GNP, also valued at 1966 prices.

Capacity GNP cannot be measured or observed directly except when the economy is operating close to the 4 percent target unemployment rate. But there is enough indirect evidence based on levels of GNP achieved when unemployment has been 4 percent in the past, on productivity trends, and so on, to justify the use of the smooth curve in Figure 1 as a crude working approximation of the recent trend of productive capacity. Moreover, the validity of the estimates for earlier years is borne out to some degree by the fact that when unemployment declined to the neighborhood of 4 percent in late 1965, actual output turned out to be very close to the estimate of productive capacity. The reader is cautioned, however, not to attach much significance to the precise values indicated by the capacity output curve but to

[5] The calculations used here are similar to those made by the Council of Economic Advisers. See the Annual Reports of the Council of Economic Advisers, January 1962 (pp. 49–53), January 1965 (p. 81), and January 1967 (p. 44). There are many problems, both conceptual and statistical, in measuring the economy's productive capacity. The intellectual basis for the Council's estimates was provided by Arthur M. Okun in his paper, "Potential GNP: Its Measurement and Significance," 1962 *Proceedings of the Business and Economic Statistics Section of the American Statistical Association*, reprinted as *Cowles Foundation Paper No. 190* (Cowles Foundation for Research in Economics, Yale University, 1963).

regard them as the center of a range of perhaps $5 billion within which the true value lies. Furthermore, the curve cannot safely be projected very far into the future, since the growth of productive capacity may change both because of essentially adventitious factors, such as alterations in the rate of growth of the labor force or in the rate of capital accumulation, and because the choice of economic policies, such as those discussed in this paper, may significantly change the growth of capacity.

What can we say about economic growth and the means of achieving it on the basis of Figure 1? To begin with, it is apparent that, starting from a situation such as existed in early 1961 when unemployment was in the neighborhood of 7 percent of the labor force and the gap between actual GNP and capacity GNP was in excess of $50 billion, a significant amount of growth in actual GNP can be achieved merely by reducing unemployment to 4 percent and bringing actual GNP up to level of capacity GNP. To illustrate, in order to reduce unemployment to the target level of 4 percent in two years' time beginning in the first quarter of 1961, we would have had to raise GNP from its actual level of $550 billion at that time to its potential level of $652 billion in the first quarter of 1963 (as shown on the smooth curve in Figure 1). This would have been an increase of about 18 percent in two years, or roughly 9 percent per year. Actually, unemployment was not reduced to the 4 percent level until the first quarter of 1966, but even with this relatively slow rate of expansion toward full employment, GNP rose from $550 billion in the first quarter of 1961 to $735 billion in the first quarter of 1966, for an average increase of about 6 percent per year.

Thus, substantial growth is possible in the short run through the elimination of unemployment when the economy is operating substantially below capacity, as was the case in 1961. Under such conditions, if unemployment is to be reduced to 4 percent of the labor force and the associated growth achieved, aggregate demand must expand sufficiently to ab-

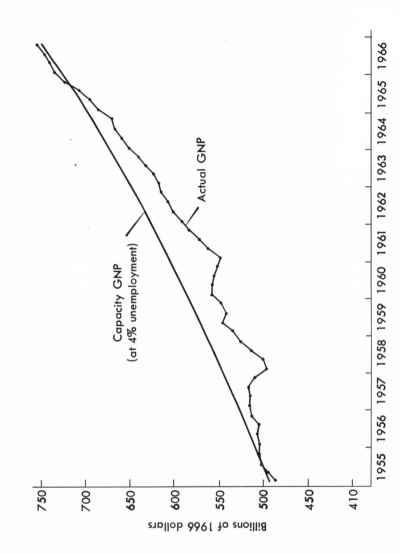

FIGURE 1

Gross National Product: Actual and Potential

sorb the quantity of goods and services that will be produced when 96 percent of the labor force is employed—or, to put it another way, aggregate demand must become equal to productive capacity as defined above. As long as demand continues to fall short of this level, producers will not find it profitable to turn out sufficient quantities of goods and services to employ 96 percent of the labor force, and unemployment will remain above 4 percent.

Eliminating transactions in materials and components to be used in further production, the total output of the economy (GNP) must necessarily be absorbed by demands which can be classified into four categories: consumer demand; business demand for new plants and equipment and additions to inventories; net export demand of foreign buyers; and government demand, Federal, state, and local. When aggregate demand is growing less rapidly than capacity, the following measures can be taken to speed up the growth of some or all of these components of demand:

(1) Taxes may be reduced, as was done in the Revenue Act of 1964, by cutting the tax rates applicable to various categories of income. The effects will depend to some extent on the exact nature of the tax-reduction measures adopted, but, in general, tax reduction will leave consumers and businesses with larger incomes after tax than previously and thereby lead directly to increases in "consumer demand" and "investment demand." These increases in demand will generate additional production of consumer goods and capital goods, thereby creating additional jobs. The additional wage incomes and business profits resulting from expanded production and employment will lead to still further consumer spending and generate additional production, employment, and income. Thus, through repeated "rounds" of additional production, income generation, and consumption spending— a process which economists call the "multiplier"—GNP will be raised by an amount in excess of the initial reduction in taxes. The available evidence suggests that a reduction of

$1 billion in individual income taxes might lead, in the course of time, to an associated rise in consumption and GNP of roughly $2 billion, thereby giving rise to a "multiplier" of about two. Beyond this, if the expansion of consumption spending produced by the cut in taxes is sufficiently rapid to narrow the gap between actual GNP and productive capacity, it will lead to a more intensive utilization of existing plant capacity and create a stimulus for businessmen to increase their spending on new plants and equipment, thus raising the "investment demand" component of GNP. This will, of course, generate additional income and employment and lead to a further increase in consumption. Although the investment effects are more difficult to estimate than the direct consumption effects referred to above, they may under some circumstances be substantial.

(2) Federal expenditures on such projects as highways, dams, and school construction may be increased. Such expenditures will directly raise GNP by adding to the "government demand" component. The added construction activity will put people to work, not only directly on the construction sites but also in factories producing materials needed in construction. As workers receive additional income in wages and salaries, and as businessmen earn additional profits from expanded production, they will increase their spending on goods and services, adding to the "consumer demand" component of GNP and stimulating additional production, employment, and income in industries producing consumer goods. Thus, through repeated "rounds" of additional production, income generation, and consumption spending similar to those set off by tax reduction, GNP will be raised by an amount in excess of the initial increase in government spending. An increase of $1 billion in government spending might lead, in the course of time, to an associated rise in consumption of roughly $1 billion, thereby producing a total rise in GNP of around $2 billion, taking account of consumption effects only, giving rise to a "multiplier" of approximately

two.[6] Moreover, as in the case of tax reduction, the rise in government spending and the associated increase in consumption may, by leading to more intensive utilization of existing productive capacity, induce businessmen to increase their expenditures on additional plant, equipment, and inventories, thus generating a still further rise in GNP.

(3) The Federal Reserve authorities may adopt a more expansionary monetary policy by, for example, expanded purchases of U.S. Government securities in the open market. Such purchases increase the cash reserves available to the commercial banks and enable the banks to expand their loans and investments and the amount of money held by the public in the form of bank deposits and currency by an amount equal to several times the additional reserves through the familiar process of bank credit expansion. Thus, bank loans will become easier to obtain, and the interest rates charged will probably be reduced. Furthermore, the expansion of credit will indirectly lower interest rates on bonds issued by private corporations to finance plant expansion as well as on bonds issued by state and local government units to finance highways and schools. Mortgage credit for the financing of new homes and installment loans for the purchase of automobiles and other consumer durable goods will become easier to obtain and less costly. As a result of these developments, some expansion can be expected to take place in those components of demand that are frequently credit-financed, including housing demand, business investment demand, and the demand for consumer durable goods. The increased demand will stimulate production, income, and employment directly, and set off the

[6] Actually, both *a priori* reasoning and empirical evidence derived from statistical models of the U.S. economy suggest that the multiplier applicable to an increase in government expenditures on goods and services is a little larger than that applicable to a reduction in taxes. The reason for this is that, in the first instance, the entire increase in government expenditures constitutes, by definition, an increase in demand for goods and services, whereas some portion of a reduction in taxes is likely to be saved so that the resulting direct increase in consumer or business demand will be somewhat smaller than the tax reduction.

same "multiplier" effects produced by an increase in government expenditures or a reduction in taxes. While it is generally agreed that measures to increase the supply of money and credit will have a stimulative effect on the economy, in the present state of knowledge it is difficult to estimate the magnitude of these effects.

Thus, when the economy is operating substantially below full employment, fiscal and monetary measures which expand aggregate demand may, by pushing the economy up to full employment, be able to produce a rather high rate of growth in the short run. Once capacity operations have been achieved, however, the growth of aggregate demand must be slowed down and brought into line with the growth of capacity if an unacceptable degree of inflation is to be avoided. That is, once full employment has been reached, the limit on economic growth is set not by the rate of expansion of aggregate demand but by the rate of growth of capacity. Of course, if full employment is to be sustained on a continuing basis, demand must grow in line with capacity—that is, along the smooth curve in Figure 1. But, under these conditions, if any further increase in the rate of growth is to be achieved without undue inflation, an acceleration in the growth of capacity itself is required.

The achievement of full employment is likely, however, to have a favorable effect on the growth of productive capacity. The productive capacity of the economy at any particular time depends upon the size of the labor force; the skill, experience, and education of the workers; the nature of the technology available and in use; the quantity and quality of social overhead capital, including communication and transportation facilities and facilities for the maintenance of the health of the population; and the size, quality, and age distribution of the stock of private capital. Thus, the rate of growth of capacity depends upon the rate of growth of the labor force; the rate at which its skill, experience, and education are improving; the rate of technological advance; and the rate of accumulation of social overhead and private capital. The achievement of full employment is itself likely to have a favorable effect on some of these forces determining the rate of growth of capacity. In this connection, two factors are likely to be particularly important.

First, the improvement in rates of utilization of existing productive facilities associated with the achievement of full employment is very likely to provide a stimulus to private investment in new plant and equipment, thereby leading to faster growth of the stock of capital. And, since the installation of equipment is often the vehicle by which new technology is introduced into productive processes, the allocation of more resources to investment should also lead to more rapid introduction of new techniques. Between 1947 and 1955, both years in which unemployment was in the neighborhood of 4 percent of the labor force, real GNP grew at a rate of 4.4 percent per year. This rate is substantially greater than the rate of growth of capacity of about 3.5 percent per annum recorded during the period 1955 to 1962. Probably one of the reasons for the more rapid growth of capacity during the early postwar period is that a substantially greater proportion of the total GNP was allocated to private capital formation in the earlier period. Between 1947 and 1955, business outlays on fixed capital ranged from 10 to 12 percent of GNP, whereas between 1958 and 1963 the ratio was consistently less than 10 percent.[7] No doubt many factors contributed to the decline of the share of national output devoted to capital accumulation, but probably one of the important reasons was that for

---

[7] Actually, the rate of growth of capacity presumably depends (among other things) on the fraction of *capacity* output used for capital formation. In the earlier postwar period unemployment was 4 percent or lower much of the time, so that actual output was more or less equal to productive capacity. From 1958 to 1963, on the other hand, unemployment consistently exceeded 4 percent and output remained well below capacity, as is indicated by the gap between the smooth curve and the broken line in Figure 1. As a result, the ratio of investment to *capacity* output declined even more relative to the earlier period than did the ratio of investment to *actual* output.

several years after 1957 markets for goods and services were consistently so weak that most firms were unable to sell at profitable prices the full output that could be produced efficiently with their existing plant capacity. As a consequence, the inducement to invest in further productive facilities was severely weakened. In 1965 and 1966, as markets strengthened, as rates of utilization of existing plant facilities rose, and as the economy moved strongly back toward full employment, investment spending took on renewed vigor, rising to 10.7 percent of GNP in 1965 and 11.2 percent in 1966. At the same time, as noted above, the rate of growth of capacity appears to have moved back up to 4 percent per year.

Second, unemployment and underutilization of productive facilities increase incentives to seek job security and the protection of limited markets through the adoption of restrictive practices which cut down the effective productive capacity of the economy and reduce its rate of growth. Labor unions seek to protect their members by engaging in "featherbedding" and resisting the introduction of improved production techniques which may eliminate jobs. Businessmen are motivated to adopt pricing policies designed to protect their existing markets and to avoid risky new ventures which might seem attractive in a period of strong and expanding markets.

Undoubtedly, the particular kinds of measures that are used to expand aggregate demand may have some effect on the fraction of national resources devoted to investment during the course of an expansion to full employment. For example, if the expansion is powered by an easy monetary policy which reduces interest rates, expanded investment may play a more important role in the expansion than will be the case if the recovery is caused by a reduction in personal income taxes to stimulate consumption or by an increase in government expenditures. Measures such as the liberalized regulations governing the tax-treatment of depreciation which were put into effect in 1962 and the 7 percent tax credit for investment enacted in the Revenue Act of 1962 may have effects somewhat similar to an easy monetary policy. But when the economy has operated below full employment for a number of years, the most important factor in strengthening the inducement to invest in new plant and equipment is an expansion of aggregate demand which will increase utilization rates of existing facilities. That is, in such circumstances, the generation of additional aggregate demand is much more important than the precise nature of the measures adopted to achieve this objective, even though these specific measures may have a second-order influence on the size of the investment component of the expansion.

POLICIES TO INCREASE PRIVATE INVESTMENT

As indicated above, when the economy is operating below full employment, we may be able to achieve rapid growth in the short run merely by adopting policies to expand aggregate demand, thereby putting existing resources more fully to use. Moreover, the very process of demand expansion which drives the economy to full employment will set up forces conducive to higher rates of investment and more rapid introduction of technological improvements, thus accelerating the growth of productive capacity and creating an atmosphere generally more favorable to long-run growth. Suppose, however, we find that growth is not rapid enough to satisfy our tastes at a time when the economy is already operating at full employment. Under these conditions, mere expansion of aggregate demand will not be able to increase the rate of growth without generating inflation. If we are to accelerate growth in these circumstances, we can only do so by reallocating resources from uses that do not contribute to growth of capacity to uses that do so contribute.

One way to increase the rate of growth of capacity under full-employment conditions would be to shift resources from the production of goods and services for current consumption to the production of capital equipment. Two steps would be needed to bring about such a shift of resources from consumption to private investment. First, it would be necessary to increase the overall rate of saving in the economy—to reduce current consumption—in order to release resources for the production of more capital goods. Second, measures would have to be taken to increase expenditures by businesses for plant and equipment in order to absorb the resources released by the increased saving. If we succeeded in accomplishing the first step—the increase in saving—but failed to achieve the second—the increase in spending on plant and equipment— the result would be not an increase in the rate of growth of productive capacity but instead the appearance of unemployment and underutilization of existing productive facilities.

There are a number of methods by which the overall saving rate might be increased, all of which would involve revisions in the tax structure. Private saving might be increased by a shift toward a less progressive tax system—that is, a reduction in taxes on high-income individuals who save a large portion of their incomes, combined with an increase in taxes on low-income persons who ordinarily save relatively little. However, there is evidence that the response of saving to *changes* in income at the margin does not vary greatly among income-size brackets, except perhaps as between the very highest and the very lowest income individuals. Thus, it would probably take a very large redistribution of income to change the aggregate amount of saving significantly. Such a massive redistribution from low-income to high-income individuals would violate accepted principles of equity in the distribution of income.

An alternative means of increasing personal saving would be the enactment of a Federal sales or expenditure tax as a partial substitute for the individual income tax. Since the sales or expenditure tax would not be levied on that portion of income that was saved, it might cause an increase in personal saving. Once again, however, such a substitution of a sales or expenditure tax for the income tax would be objectionable to many people, because it would reduce the progressivity of the overall Federal tax structure.

Various other tax devices for stimulating personal or business saving could be devised, but in most cases they would probably be found objectionable on the grounds that they would either be inequitable in their effect on the distribution of income after taxes or would distort private decisions concerning the use of resources. Furthermore, in the present state of economic knowledge, it would be difficult to predict the magnitude of the increase in personal or business saving that would be caused by such measures.

Probably the best means of increasing total saving in the economy would be a general increase in taxes or a reduction of the Federal Government's non-investment expenditures for the purpose of creating a Federal budget surplus. Such a surplus would mean that the Federal Government was contributing to total saving in the economy by withdrawing more dollars from the spending stream through taxation than it was injecting through expenditures.[8] A Federal budget surplus would release resources for private investment in the same way as would an increase in private saving. Whether the surplus should be created by raising taxes or by reducing government non-investment expenditures would depend upon whether it was felt to be socially more desirable to reduce private consumption or public consumption.[9]

[8] If the Federal Government was running a budget deficit at the time and reduced the size of its deficit either by increasing taxes or by cutting expenditures, the effect would be the same as would be produced if an equal increase in taxes or reduction in expenditures created a surplus or increased the size of an existing surplus. Reduction of an existing deficit would mean that the Federal Government was absorbing less private saving than before, thereby leaving more available for private investment.

[9] A reduction of Federal investment expenditures—on such activities as education, highways, and so on—would, of course, also increase public saving through the Federal budget. Whether an increase in public

If taxes were increased to create a budget surplus, equity could be maintained by distributing the increase in taxation among income brackets in an appropriate way.[10] Since consumption has generally been within the range of 93 to 95 percent of personal disposable income in recent years, a tax increase that was reasonably evenly distributed among income brackets could be expected to reduce personal saving by 5 to 7 percent of the tax increase, thus leading to an overall increase in saving, at the then existing level of income, of about 93 to 95 percent of the increase. A cut in Federal non-investment expenditures on goods and services, on the other hand, would increase the Federal budget surplus dollar for dollar without directly depressing private saving, thereby increasing total saving in the economy by the full amount of the cut. Thus, adjustments in the overall level of taxation or in Federal expenditures would have the advantage over tax devices designed to increase private saving of being both more equitable and more predicable in terms of effects on total saving.

As indicated above, measures designed to increase saving—

---

saving produced in this way would serve to increase the rate of growth would depend upon whether the productivity of the additional private investment made possible by the increased saving was greater or smaller than the productivity of the Federal Government investment projects which were eliminated.

[10] In a growing economy, it may be possible to achieve the budget surpluses needed for a still further acceleration of growth without actually raising tax *rates* (or reducing expenditures). Assuming a 4 percent growth of real GNP and a 2 percent annual rise in the average prices of the goods and services included in GNP, capacity GNP at current prices would rise by about 6 percent per year. Thus, under full-employment conditions, starting from present levels, GNP would rise by about $45 billion a year, and with our present tax system, taxes would increase by about 25 percent of this amount, or about $11 billion a year. Unless Federal expenditures were to rise by this amount or unless tax rates were periodically reduced, the budget would show a steadily increasing surplus at full employment. Thus, one possible strategy for accelerating growth would be to limit the secular rise of Federal expenditures while taking monetary or fiscal measures to increase private investment to match the budget surpluses automatically generated by the secular growth of tax revenues.

that is, to release resources from the production of goods and services for current consumption—would need to be accompanied by measures to stimulate an equal amount of additional investment spending. Otherwise, the result would be reduced employment rather than accelerated growth.[11]

One measure that might be taken to stimulate private investment would be to use the budget surplus resulting from the increase in taxes or the reduction in Federal expenditures to retire a portion of the outstanding public debt. By retiring debt, the Federal Government would be putting the funds collected through the budget surplus into the capital market, thereby bringing down interest rates and making the funds available for the financing of private investment.

While the use of surplus funds collected through the Federal budget for debt retirement would be desirable in itself and would help to a limited extent to spur private investment, debt retirement alone would not generate sufficient investment to absorb the full amount of resources released by the initial reduction in consumption spending. That is, one dollar of debt retirement will not generate a full dollar of additional private investment. The reason is that a decline in interest rates will cause individuals and business concerns to increase their holdings of money balances. That is, a portion of the additional dollars injected into the capital market by debt retirement will be "hoarded" in the form of additional money holdings rather than being spent for private investment. In fact, it appears that the demand for money holdings is sufficiently responsive to a decline in interest rates to cancel out a substantial portion of the effect of debt retirement. In other words, an increase in taxes or a reduction in Federal expenditures, combined with the use of the resulting budget surplus to retire an equivalent amount of public debt, would,

[11] Paradoxically, if appropriate measures were not taken to stimulate investment, the measures designed to increase saving would reduce income, and this would *depress* saving. When all the adjustments had been completed, therefore, total saving might differ very little from its initial level, but income and employment would be lower.

in all probability, have a net deflationary effect on the economy, thereby causing a reduction in income and employment.

One way to supplement the expansionary effects of using the budget surplus to retire debt would be for the Federal Reserve System to shift simultaneously toward an easier monetary policy. For example, the Federal Reserve could, in effect, retire *additional* publicly held debt through open-market purchases of U.S. Government securities, thereby lowering interest rates directly and also adding to the supply of cash reserves of the commercial banks and permitting them to engage in a further expansion of money and credit.

Under some circumstances, a shift toward an easier monetary policy by the Federal Reserve would be the logical means of supplementing the use of the budget surplus to retire debt as a means of stimulating private investment. However, since the available evidence suggests that private investment is only moderately sensitive to declining interest rates and increased availability of credit, the Federal Reserve System should be prepared to use its full powers to bring about the needed increase in private investment. To the extent that the Federal Reserve failed to act with sufficient vigor, the result would be deflationary, leading to reduced income and employment rather than the desired increase in investment and productive capacity.

Under the conditions that have existed in the last few years —and probably will continue for some time to come—a sharp reduction in interest rates for the purpose of stimulating private investment might seriously increase the U.S. balance-of-payments deficit and lead to a loss of gold. This is because a decline in U.S. interest rates relative to those prevailing in foreign markets would be very likely to cause an outflow of private capital.

What we have described above is what has come to be an almost standard post-Keynesian prescription for increasing the rate of economic growth: a shift toward a tighter fiscal policy to generate a budget surplus through increased taxation or reduced government expenditures, combined with a shift toward an easier monetary policy to spur private investment. However, if monetary policy is constrained by the balance-of-payments situation, as has been the case in the last few years, the second half of the prescription may prove to be impossible to put into effect. If this is the case, a policy of stimulating economic growth will require the use of some measures other than easy money to produce the needed increase in private investment.

If easy money and reduced interest rates should in fact prove to be either inadequate or impossible, there are various tax-incentive devices that might be employed to increase private investment. The most straightforward of these would be a reduction in corporate income tax rates, which would stimulate investment in plant and equipment by leaving corporations with larger after-tax incomes for the internal financing of investment, and also by increasing the prospective after-tax returns on newly installed facilities, and thereby strengthening incentives to invest. An alternative device would be a liberalization of the regulations governing the treatment of depreciation for tax purposes. By allowing faster write-offs of plants, machinery, and equipment, liberalized depreciation would increase the so-called "cash flow" of internal funds for financing investment and would also strengthen investment incentives by increasing the prospective rate of return on new investment. Still a third possibility would be an increase in the investment tax credit enacted in the Revenue Act of 1962 and liberalized in the Revenue Act of 1964. Such a tax credit has somewhat the same effect as would be produced by a reduction in the initial cost of eligible productive facilities and hence makes investment more attractive to business.[12]

[12] The Revenue Act of 1962 allowed the investor a credit against income tax amounting to 7 percent of investment in eligible assets (including, in general, machinery and equipment but not buildings) having a life of eight years or more (with smaller percentage credits for investments with lives of between four and eight years). Originally, the tax credit had to be deducted from the base on which depreciation was

In addition, to the extent that it reduces taxes, the credit provides firms with additional internal funds to finance investment. Of the three devices, the last one—an increase in the investment credit—has the advantage of being pinpointed most sharply toward the stimulation of investment, and it therefore seems preferable to the others.

By appropriate adjustments in fiscal policy—and, to the extent that the balance-of-payments situation permits, in monetary policy—it should be possible in the course of time to increase the proportion of national resources employed in private capital formation and thereby to raise to some extent the rate of economic growth. But such a policy adjustment is delicate and risky and should be pursued cautiously. If the fiscal and monetary measures that are designed to increase investment do not have the desired effects, the result will be unemployment and underutilization of existing productive capacity—and probably reduced investment—rather than increased growth of capacity.

The relation of budget deficits and surpluses to economic growth is generally rather poorly understood. It is often said that exponents of the vigorous use of fiscal policy for the maintenance of economic stability believe that continuing budget deficits year after year serve to stimulate growth. This is simply not the position held by the more sophisticated exponents of an active fiscal policy. It is true that when the economy is suffering from unemployment, a reduction in taxes or an increase in Federal expenditures, leading to a budget deficit, may be desirable as a means of increasing aggregate demand and raising economic activity to the full employment level. But, as explained above, if the objective being

---

calculated; as a result, the effect on investment was exactly the same as that of a reduction in the price of the asset by the tax-credit percentage. The Revenue Act of 1964 liberalized the credit by eliminating the provision requiring that the credit be deducted from the depreciation base. Thus, at present the tax credit has a stronger stimulating effect on investment than would be produced by an equal percentage reduction in the price of the asset.

sought is long-run economic growth—that is, growth of productive capacity—budget surpluses, not budget deficits, will, by increasing aggregate national saving, contribute to that end, provided the surpluses are accompanied by monetary or fiscal action which increases private investment sufficiently to employ all the saving, including the surplus, that will be forthcoming at full employment. That is, if effective stimuli to investment can be put into effect, a policy of surplus financing rather than deficit financing is generally recognized by economists as being favorable to long-run economic growth.

OTHER POLICIES FOR GROWTH

In addition to the policy adjustments discussed above to increase private investment, there are other measures involving the use of fiscal policy which might be taken to speed economic growth. Most of these measures would involve either increased spending on government programs which would increase the future productive capacity of the economy or the use of tax incentives to encourage private activities—other than investment in plant and equipment—directed at that end.

Policies to make the labor market work more efficiently should be placed high on the agenda of programs aimed at increasing the effective productive capacity of the economy. Increased appropriations to enable the United States Employment Service to expand its activities in disseminating job information for the benefit of workers seeking employment, the use of Federal subsidies or perhaps credits under the individual income tax to reduce the cost to workers of moving from one locality to another to accept employment, and greatly increased Federal expenditures on programs for the training and retraining of the unemployed would be helpful. Combined with efforts—through such devices as the so-called "wage-price guideposts" of the Council of Economic Advisers

—to prevent inflationary excesses in collective bargaining, measures of this kind might permit the unemployment rate to be reduced below 4 percent without creating excessive inflationary pressure. While not necessarily increasing the *percentage rate of growth* of productive capacity, such policies would, if effective, produce a "once-and-for-all" increment to capacity, thereby permitting the growth curve of capacity to be redrawn at a higher level, corresponding perhaps to a 3 percent rather than a 4 percent unemployment rate. Since they would enable the economy to produce larger quantities of goods and services not only currently but in the future, these measures should be classified as growth policies. And, since they would reduce the economic distress and disillusionment created by unemployment, they would be valuable measures from the standpoint of social policy as well.

Expenditures on research and development which increase both the size and quality of the available stock of technical knowledge—that is, which expand the scope of the "book of recipes" for combining resources to produce goods and services—are of critical importance for growth. The benefits to society from private expenditures on research and development often cannot be fully captured by those who put up the money to finance the required research activities. This is especially true of basic research of potentially wide applicability, but which may not lead to an immediately marketable product. That is to say, the social benefits of research and development expenditures often exceed the benefits accruing to the private sponsors of such activities. Under these conditions, if the full costs of research and development programs are borne by their private sponsors, the activities of these sponsors will be carried only to the point where private benefits and private costs are brought to equality at the margin, and the resources devoted to research and development will be smaller than would be desirable from the standpoint of society as a whole. This is a classic example of a situation where the free market does not perform its allocative function with optimal efficiency, and some form of government intervention is therefore in order.

The Federal Government's expenditures in support of research and development quadrupled—from $3.1 billion to $12.4 billion—between 1954 and 1964. However, a large portion of its research and development effort is related to the improvement of defense technology and the development of the space program and has limited direct applicability in the private economy.[13] Indeed, Federal support of basic research —the area into which private market incentives are least likely to channel an adequate volume of resources—amounted to only about $1.5 billion in 1964. In view of the probably wide disparity between the social benefits of expenditures on research and development and their costs to private sponsors, increased Federal expenditures in support of such activities— especially basic research—would be desirable and would contribute to economic growth.

Another method of increasing expenditures on research and development would be to provide tax incentives to business firms for such expenditures. For example, a tax credit similar to the 7 percent credit for investment in machinery and equipment enacted in the Revenue Act of 1962, could be given for research and development spending.[14] By reducing the effec-

---

[13] Knowledge accumulated as a result of defense and space activities does have some private applications. This knowledge is certainly not being disseminated and used to the greatest possible extent at the present time. Expanded efforts by the Federal Government to make available to private users some of the technical knowledge accumulated as a result of defense-and-space-connected research would contribute to economic growth.

[14] Taxpayers are permitted to deduct outlays for research as current expenses in computing their income tax liabilities. This favorable tax treatment may not, however, be applied to long-lived equipment used for research; the cost of such equipment must be recovered by depreciation allowances spread over its life. As a means of stimulating research and development in the interest of economic growth, the tax reform program proposed by President Kennedy in 1963 contained a provision that would have permitted the taxpayer to deduct the cost of research equipment as an expense for tax purposes in the year in which the

tive cost to business of research activities, such a tax credit should be capable of providing a strong stimulus to private research. Any tax credit proposal should disallow credits for such activities as market research and sales promotion, because their contribution to economic growth is likely to be minimal and because, in any case, private market incentives are likely to call them forth in adequate amounts.

Public investment in such fields as health, education, highway construction, the conservation and development of natural resources, and urban planning and development have a vital role to play in spurring economic growth. Accordingly, within limits at least, increased Federal expenditures in these areas —or perhaps grants to state and local government units to permit them to increase such expenditures—should be an important part of any program aimed at increasing the rate of growth. In defining public investment, it is important to avoid emphasizing the accumulation of "bricks and mortar"—public buildings, highways, dams, and so on—and in the process neglect those areas of public investment which do not take this form. Most students of growth believe that outlays for the improvement of human resources are capable of yielding spectacularly high returns. Programs for improving health and for education and training are of special importance. Investment in the improvement of human resources includes not only outlays for the construction of physical facilities, such as hospitals and schools, but also expenditures required for the current operation of medical and educational institutions, such as the payment of teachers' salaries. The criterion for defining investment should be not the acquisition of physical assets such as buildings and equipment, but rather the existence of a future payoff in terms of increased productivity. Moreover, expenditures for health and education yield benefits in the

---

equipment was acquired. However, this provision was rejected by the Congress and was not included in the tax reform program as finally enacted in the Revenue Act of 1964.

form of greater happiness and increased personal fulfillment, benefits which are by no means fully reflected in the GNP that is used as a material index of economic growth.

Increased government spending on research and development and on public investment, as well as tax credits which succeed in stimulating private outlays on research and development, will, if introduced at a time when the economy is already at full employment, need to be accompanied by measures designed to depress some other kinds of expenditures if inflation is to be avoided. That is, under conditions of full employment, policies designed to stimulate growth-generating expenditures—whether these expenditures be private or public and whether they be for investment in physical facilities, for research and development to improve technology, or for the improvement of human resources—should be accompanied by measures designed to increase saving (*i.e.*, reduce consumption) in order to release resources to be used for their fulfillment. Thus, the measures designed to increase saving—private or public—discussed earlier in this paper are a necessary accompaniment of policies to stimulate growth-oriented expenditures, whether such expenditures be in the private or in the public sector.

Those who favor an expanded program of public investment aimed at the development of the economy and the improvement of human resources often advocate the adoption of a so-called "capital budget" by the Federal Government. In a full-fledged capital budget, government expenditures would be classified between capital outlays (which should be defined to include all expenditures yielding future benefits) on the one hand, and expenditures yielding only current benefits on the other. According to the capital-budget principle, taxes should cover expenditures yielding current benefits together with debt interest and amortization, while capital outlays should be financed by borrowing. This procedure is supposed to have the advantage of spreading the cost of financing capital expenditures, in the form of interest and amortization, over the life of the facilities acquired so that the persons who, as a group, benefit from the added productivity of the facilities are required to bear the costs. In addition, a parallel is sometimes drawn between the principles underlying a public capital budget and the tenets often accepted as sound for private finance. The argument runs that just as it is regarded as proper for a business firm or a family to borrow money for the purpose of acquiring long-lasting assets such as an automobile, a house, a store, or a plant, so should it be viewed as appropriate for the government to borrow to finance the construction of a dam, a highway, or outlays for the education of its citizens. Conversely, it would be improper for the government to borrow to finance outlays yielding only current benefits just as it would be improper for a family to borrow to buy food or clothing. Unfortunately, even if this somewhat Puritanical theory of private finance is accepted—note that it is an ethical rather than an economic theory—there is no reason why the same principles should be applied to governments, especially the Federal Government. Indeed, there are two extremely serious objections to the theory as applied to the Federal budget.

First, acceptance of the theory of the capital budget as outlined above might at times interfere seriously with the maintenance of full employment. When the forces of private demand are particularly weak, the needs of economic stabilization may require the Federal Government to reduce taxes or increase expenditures to such an extent that tax revenues would be inadequate to cover even that portion of Federal expenditures yielding only current benefits. On the other hand, at times when private demand is exceptionally buoyant and the economy is therefore threatened by inflation, the maintenance of economic stability may require such a large increase in taxes or reduction in expenditures that tax revenues will be more than sufficient to cover all Federal expenditures including capital outlays. Indeed, it will only happen by accident—if ever—that the Federal budget deficit that would occur when tax revenues were just sufficient to cover expenditures yielding current benefits would be the appropriate budgetary situation from the standpoint of economic stabilization. In other words, the capital budget is almost certain to come into serious conflict with the overriding principles of countercyclical fiscal policy.

Second, the principle underlying the capital budget is not even acceptable in terms of its effects on the allocation of resources, at least to one who, like myself, accepts the idea that the government has an important role to play in influencing the rate of economic growth. If the government wishes to accelerate growth, it may be quite inappropriate to finance public investment by borrowing, since such borrowing may drive up interest rates and reduce private investment which also contributes to growth; rather, from the standpoint of optimal growth policy, it may be desirable to finance government capital outlays by an increase in personal taxes designed to release from private consumption the resources needed for the government's investment program. Indeed, an effective program aimed at the twin objectives of stability and growth requires that the whole complex of monetary and fiscal policies be the subject of flexible adjustments and be kept continuously under review. Dogmatic rules which connect certain kinds of expenditures with certain means of finance are likely to prove unsatisfactory because they prevent appropriate policy adjustments.

Arguments that justify Federal deficits to the extent that they result from borrowing to finance public capital outlays by analogy to so-called "sound" tenets of private finance are generally fallacious. The soundness of the Federal Government's credit rests not on the value of its assets but on the strength of the economy, its taxable capacity, and, ultimately, on the Government's power to create money. If needed to maintain high employment and optimal resource allocation, borrowing and deficit spending to finance *current* government expenditures are perfectly appropriate—indeed, if the alternative is widespread unemployment, failure to accept the necessary borrowing and deficit financing should be roundly condemned as a failure of the Government to live up to its responsibility for the maintenance of a sound economy. Nor should the capital budget be favored, as it certainly has been by some people and at some times, as a device for justifying deficits that are required to keep the economy operating at full employment. It is better to make the case for deficit financing when needed for economic stabilization on the basis of correct fiscal-policy reasoning rather than to use expedient arguments to justify it by means of false analogies to private finance.[15]

CONCLUDING REMARKS

I have discussed a number of ways in which changes in the level and structure of taxation, changes in the level and composition of Federal expenditures, and changes in monetary policy might be capable of expediting growth of real output in the United States. Apart from the possibility of accelerating growth in the short run by putting to work resources that are currently idle, nearly all of the measures discussed require significant reallocations of resources—the application of measures to reduce the use of resources for current consumption combined with measures to absorb these released resources into uses that increase the total productive power of the economy, such as private investment in plant and equipment, increased activity in the field of research and development, increased public investment in physical facilities such as high-

[15] Although a capital budget procedure of the kind outlined seems unwise, it is perfectly appropriate—indeed desirable—for the Federal budget to present a breakdown of expenditures between those yielding benefits primarily in the future and those yielding benefits primarily in the current year. This breakdown is in fact provided in Special Analysis D of the Federal budget. (See *The Budget of the United States Government for the Fiscal Year Ending June 30, 1967*, pp. 406–25).

ways and development of natural resources, and increased investment in human resources. All of these policies for promoting economic growth require us to make choices: We must decide the extent to which we are willing to give up the current enjoyment of the fruits of the economy in the form of consumption for the purpose of accumulating additional capital of one kind or another which will increase the capacity of the economy to produce goods and services in the future. Moreover, it should be understood that the policy adjustments needed to produce a deliberate speed-up of growth are rather sophisticated, uncertain as to effects, and difficult to put into operation. On the basis of the evidence currently available, it is extremely difficult to predict the magnitude of the effects likely to be produced on the growth of the productive capacity of the economy by any particular measure, such as increased private investment, or by any combination of measures. As a consequence, it is vitally important that we have in our arsenal of fiscal policies instruments that can be employed quickly and flexibly to adjust aggregate demand to whatever the growth rate of capacity turns out to be, if we are to be able to maintain full employment on a continuing basis.

It is almost certain that the optimal way to increase economic growth is by the use of some combination of the proposals discussed above: to allocate some additional resources to private investment, some to the expansion of research and development activities, some to increased public investment in physical facilities, and some to the improvement of human resources. The general principle that should underlie selection of the optimal mix of policies for achieving a given growth objective is to carry each of the various growth-generating activities to the point where the marginal social productivities of all of them are equated. Then, having decided the optimal combination of these activities for each given increment to the growth rate, the total amount of resources withdrawn from current consumption for use in promoting growth-oriented activities should be decided on the basis of our willingness as a nation—as reflected in the decisions of our policy makers chosen through democratic political processes—to give up current consumption in exchange for future consumption.

Unfortunately, while it is a relatively simple matter to state, at least crudely, the principles that should underlie the selection of an optimal growth policy, it is, as a practical matter, impossible to make such a rational calculation in the present state of knowledge. Opinions differ substantially concerning the relative magnitudes of the contributions to economic growth that have been made by private investment, technological change, education, and so on; and it is possible to marshal the evidence in such a way as to support a fairly wide range of estimates with respect to these contributions. Of course, further empirical work on the sources of economic growth may in time enable us to make better judgments concerning the contributions of different kinds of growth-promoting activities. For the present, however, about the best that can be said is that a combination of measures aimed at all of the main sources of economic growth simultaneously is probably better than single-minded concentration on one source such as private investment. But, with respect to the relative emphasis to be placed on different kinds of activities, the judgments of qualified students of growth differ, and no clear choice seems possible. In other words, in the present state of knowledge, the choice of an appropriate combination of policies for promoting economic growth is an art rather than a science.

Part IV

Economic Growth as an Objective of Government Policy

BY

James Tobin

* I am greatly indebted to my colleagues at the Cowles Foundation, especially Tjalling Koopmans, Arthur Okun, and E. S. Phelps, for clarifying many of the questions discussed in this paper. But they do not necessarily share my opinions, and they certainly share no responsibility for my mistakes.

In recent years economic growth has come to occupy an exalted position in the hierarchy of goals of government policy, both in the United States and abroad, both in advanced and in less-developed countries, both in centrally controlled and decentralized economies. National governments set themselves target growth rates in such diverse economies as the Soviet Union, Yugoslavia, India, Sweden, France, Japan —and even in the United Kingdom and the United States, where the targets indicate dissatisfaction with past performance. Growth is an international goal, too. The Organization for Economic Cooperation and Development aims at a 50 percent increase in the collective gross output of the Atlantic Community over the current decade.

Growth has become a good word. And the better a word becomes, the more it is invoked to bless a variety of causes and the more it loses specific meaning. At least in professional economic discussion, we need to give a definite and distinctive meaning to growth as a policy objective. Let it be neither a new synonym for good things in general nor a fashionable way to describe other economic objectives. Let growth be something it is possible to oppose as well as to favor, depending on judgments of social priorities and opportunities.

I

In essence, the question of growth is nothing new, but a new disguise for an age-old issue, one which has always intrigued and preoccupied economists—the present versus the future. How should society divide its resources between current needs and pleasures and those of next year, next decade, next generation?

The choice can be formalized in a way that makes clear what is essentially at stake. A *consumption path* or *program* for an economy describes its rate of consumption at every time point beginning now and extending indefinitely into the future. Not all imaginable consumption paths are feasible. At any moment, future possibilities are limited by our inherited stocks of productive resources and technological knowledge and by our prospects for autonomous future increase in these stocks. Of feasible paths, some dominate others: *i.e.,* path A dominates B if consumption along path A exceeds consumption along path B at every point of time. I hope I will incur no one's wrath by asserting that in almost everyone's value scheme more is better than less (or certainly not worse), at least if we are careful to specify more or less of what. If this assertion is accepted, the interesting choices are between undominated or efficient feasible paths, *e.g.,* between a pair A and C, where A promises more consumption at some points in time but less at others (see Figure 1). In particular, I take growthmanship to be advocacy of paths that promise more consumption later in return for less earlier.

But growthmanship means more than that. Growthmen are usually willing to throw the weight of the government onto the scales in order to tip the balance in favor of the future. Here they fly in the face of a doctrinal tradition of considerable strength both in economics and in popular ideology. Does not the market so coordinate the free, decentralized decisions of individuals between present and future so as to reach an optimal social choice? Is not any government intervention in favor of growth, therefore, bound to tilt the scales toward the future to a degree that society does not "really" want?

FIGURE 1

Alternative Consumption Paths

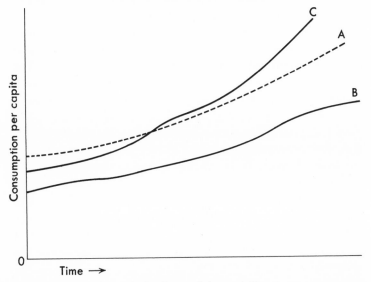

A dominates B but not C.

The basic question raised by advocates of faster growth may be further formalized to emphasize this issue. Assuming that the economy is now on a feasible and undominated consumption path, the desirability of deviating from it can be expressed in the language of interest rates and present values. Any feasible and efficient path, including the prevailing path, implies two sets of interest rates. One, which we may call the *time preference* set, expresses the society's marginal rates of substitution as consumers between consumption at one date and consumption at another date. This set answers questions like the following: Given society's consumption prospect, how much increase in consumption five years or fifty years or *t* years from now is worth the loss of a dollar's worth of consumption today? The rates implied by the answers need not all be the same. The other set, which we may call the *technological* set, expresses the opportunities which present and prospective technology offer the society for marginal substitutions of consumption at one date for consumption at another. This set answers questions like the following: Given the consumption path, by how much could consumption be increased five years or fifty years or *t* years from now by the resources released from a dollar's worth of consumption today? Again, the rates can vary with time. A sacrifice in current consumption may yield, say, 10 percent per year if its fruits are taken five years from now, but 20 percent—or 2 percent—if they are taken fifty years from now.

A small, proposed feasible deviation from the existing path can in principle be tested as follows: Calculate the present values of the proposed deviations in consumption, negative and positive, discounting them by the *time preference* set of interest rates. If the sum is positive, the proposed deviation is worthwhile. If it is zero or negative, it is not worthwhile. We know that this sum will not be positive if it happens that the *time preference* and *technological* interest rates are identical.

Evidently growthmen believe that the two sets diverge in such a way that society would give a positive present value to feasible increases in future consumption purchased at the expense of current and near-future consumption. Their opponents think the contrary. Many of them have faith in the capital markets and believe there is a presumption that these markets make the two sets of rates equal.

I I

This is the heart of the issue, I believe, and I shall return to it later in this paper. First, however, I must discuss some questions raised by the formulation of the growth issue which

I have just tried to sketch. What is the relationship between growth and other objectives of economic policy, in particular, full employment of resources? Are there some noneconomic reasons for accelerating growth, reasons which this formulation excludes or evades? Exactly what is the "consumption" whose path is to be chosen? Finally, *can* government successfully influence the growth path?

1. *Growth vs. Full Employment.* To accelerate growth is not the same thing as to increase the utilization of existing resources, manpower, and capital capacity. In the formulation sketched above, a consumption path with underutilization is dominated or inefficient. By putting the idle resources to work, consumption can be increased *both* now and in the future. The same is true of other measures to improve the efficiency of allocation of resources. We can all agree, I presume, on the desirability of growth measures free of any cost. If that is the meaning of growth policy, there is no issue.

For short periods of time, stepping up the utilization of capacity can increase the recorded rate of growth of output and consumption. But over the decades, fluctuations in the utilization of capacity will have a minor influence compared to the growth of capacity itself. To express the same point somewhat differently, the subject of economic growth refers mainly to supply, or capacity to produce, rather than to demand. In the short run, accelerating the growth of demand for goods and services can, by increasing the rate of utilization of capacity, speed the growth of output. But in the long run, output and real demand cannot grow faster than capacity. If monetary demand is made to set a faster pace, it will be frustrated by a rate of inflation that cuts real demand down to size.

Public policy affecting aggregate demand should be aimed at maintaining a desired rate of utilization of capacity. Economists and other citizens will differ on how high their rate should be, because they differ in the weights they attach to additional employment and output, on the one hand, and to the risks of faster price inflation, on the other. But however this balance is struck, monetary and fiscal policies can in principle hit the target utilization rate just as well whether the economy's capacity is growing at 5 percent or 3 percent or 0 percent.

Full employment is, therefore, not a reason for faster economic growth; each is an objective in its own right. In an economy suffering from low rates of utilization of manpower and capital resources, accelerating the growth of aggregate demand may well be the need of the hour. But this ought not be considered growth policy in the more fundamental sense. Tax reduction today has sufficient justification as a means of expanding demand and raising the rate of utilization. It is probably an unfortunate confusion to bill it as a growth measure, too.

I do not mean, of course, that the rate of growth of the economy's capacity is in practice wholly independent of its rate of utilization. In principle they may be independent. Demand can be expanded in ways that do not accelerate—indeed, may even retard—the growth in capacity itself. But as a rule, some of the output resulting from an increase in utilization will be used in ways that expand future capacity. Thus the Great Depression deprived the nation and the world of investment as well as consumption; we, as well as our fathers, bear the cost. The tax reduction of 1964–65, even though its major impact was to stimulate consumption, nonetheless substantially increased the share of national capacity devoted to capital accumulation. It is in this sense that it can be called a growth measure. But there may be ways to expand demand and utilization to the same degree while at the same time providing both more stimulus for and more economic room for capacity-building uses of resources now idle.

2. *Noneconomic reasons for growth.* Economic growth may be a national objective for noneconomic reasons, for national prestige or national strength or national purpose.

No doubt much of the recent dissatisfaction with U.S.

growth is motivated by unfavorable comparisons with other countries, especially the Soviet Union. If current rates are mechanically extrapolated, it is easy to calculate that the U.S. will not be first in international statistical comparisons in our great-grandchildren's textbooks. Presumably the American nation could somehow stand and even rationalize this blow to our national pride, even as we survive quadrennial defeats by Russian hordes in the Olympics. At any rate, it is not for professional economists to advise the country to act differently just to win a race in statistical yearbooks. The cold war will not be so easily won, or lost, or ended.

International competition in growth may, however, be of importance in the battle for prestige and allegiance among the "uncommitted" and less developed countries. These nations place a high premium on rapid economic progress. They will not—so the argument runs—choose the democratic way in preference to communism, or market economies in preference to centrally directed economies, unless our institutions show by example that they can outperform rival systems. A political psychologist rather than an economist should evaluate this claim. But it has several apparent weaknesses: (a) Rate of growth is not the only dimension of economic performance by which our society will be judged by outside observers. Equality of opportunity and of condition; humanity, understanding, and generosity in relation to less privileged people in our own society and abroad—these are perhaps more important dimensions. (b) The U.S. is not the only non-communist economy. The examples of Western Europe (in particular the contrast of Western to Eastern Germany) and Japan are more relevant to the rest of the world, and they give convincing evidence of the economic vitality of free societies. (c) What is much more important is a demonstration that an *underdeveloped* country can progress rapidly under democratic auspices. Without this kind of demonstration, faster growth of affluence in already affluent societies may cause more disaffection than admiration.

On the score of national strength, there is a case for growth. But it is more subtle than the facile association of military power with generalized civilian economic capacity. Nuclear technology has made this connection looser than ever. A country is not necessarily stronger than another just because it has a higher GNP. Great productive capacity may have been the decisive reserve of military strength in the last two world wars, but nowadays it is useless if it remains unmobilized until the cataclysmic buttons are pushed. A country with smaller GNP can be as strong or even stronger, if it persistently allocates enough of its GNP to military purposes. And in the age of overkill, apparently there can be a point of saturation.

Should we grow faster to be better prepared to meet possible future needs for output for military purposes—or for other uses connected with national foreign policy? If we do not, we will have to meet such needs when they arise by depriving other claimants on national production, principally consumption, at the time. But in order to grow faster, we have to deprive these claimants now. Hence the national power argument seems to boil down to the economist's calculation after all, *i.e.*, to the terms of trade between current and future consumption.

But there is an important exception. Some hazards are great enough to bias our choice to favor the future over the present, to accept less favorable payoffs than we otherwise would. We might conceivably be challenged one day to a duel of overriding priority, involving all-out commitment of resources to military uses, foreign aid, space adventures, or all of these together. A high GNP might be the difference between victory and defeat, rather than the difference between more or less consumption. In other words, this contingency is one that could be met only by sacrifices of consumption in advance, not by sacrifices at the time.

As for national purpose, it is surely conceivable that a growth target could inspire, galvanize, and unite the nation.

But it is not the only objective that could serve this purpose, nor is it necessarily the best candidate.

3. *Growth in What?* The formulation of the growth issue sketched above presents it as a choice among available *consumption* paths. The concentration on consumption deserves some elaboration and explanation—especially because growth performance and aspiration are popularly expressed in terms of gross or net national product.

Some of the noneconomic reasons for favoring faster growth also suggest that GNP is the relevant measure, especially if it is the most usual and visible measure. But as economists, we would make welfare or utility depend on consumption. We would require the investment part of GNP to derive its value from the future consumption it supports. After all, a future in which the rate of growth of GNP reaches fantastic heights has no appeal if the fruits of the achievement are never consumed. We must heed the "Golden Rule" of capital accumulation— there is a saving ratio and a corresponding capital intensity that maximize consumption. Persistent saving in excess of the Rule makes GNP higher but consumption lower.[1]

Neither GNP nor consumption, as ordinarily measured, counts leisure. Yet I do not understand advocates of faster growth to be taking a stand in favor of goods and services priced in the market and against leisure. Should the trend toward shorter hours, longer vacations, and earlier retirements accelerate, the rate of growth of consumption, as measured in the national accounts, might decline. But a decline for this reason should not bother a growth-oriented economist. *The Affluent Society* to the contrary notwithstanding, the conventional wisdom of economics was long since liberated from the fallacy that only produced goods and services yield utility and welfare. Economists do have prejudices against biasing the price system in favor of leisure and against forcing the leisure

[1] E. S. Phelps, "The Golden Rule of Accumulation," *American Economic Review*, September 1961, Vol. LI, pp. 638–42.

of involuntary unemployment on anyone. But those are other matters. The consumption whose growth path concerns us should include leisure valued at the real wage. Needless to say, it should also allow for consumption goods and services provided by government.

Finally, is the relevant measure aggregate consumption or consumption per capita? Do we discharge our obligation to the next generation if we enable them to enjoy the same aggregate consumption, even though there will be more of them to share it? Should we, on the other hand, sacrifice today in order to raise per capita consumption half a century from now just because there will then be more consumers? Or should generations count in some sense equally regardless of size? These are not easy questions for the social philosopher, but revealed social preferences lean towards *per capita* consumption. Presumably we do not value increase in population for its own sake. We might if sheer numbers were important for national power. But in general we are content to leave population trends to free choice; indeed, we seek to enlarge parents' ability to limit births at their discretion. Neither immigration nor subsidies for child-bearing are advanced as growth proposals. In the world at large, certainly, the commonly accepted aim is to retard the growth of population, not to accelerate it.[2]

4. *Government's Power to Influence Growth.* I come now to the question of whether the government can influence growth, even if we wish it to. The growth objective is commonly framed in terms of an exponential growth rate. Those who advocate measures to promote growth frequently are expressing a preference for a higher per annum rate of growth, for 4 percent or 5 percent instead of 3 percent or 3.5 percent.

---

[2] For discussion of this question, see T. C. Koopmans, "On the Concept of Optimal Economic Growth," Cowles Foundation Discussion Paper, No. 163, 1963, presented at a joint session of the American Economic Association and the Econometric Society on "Intertemporal Economic Theory," in the Boston Meetings, December 1963.

But the thrust of much recent theorizing and model-building is that in the really long run we have no choice about the growth rate.[3] The long-run growth rates of GNP and aggregate consumption are exogenously determined by the growth of the labor force and the progress of technology. Or, to express the same conclusion somewhat differently, the rates of growth of productivity per man and of consumption per capita are in the long run controlled by the rate of advance of technology. According to these models, there are various hypothetical paths which share the exogenously determined rate. These paths differ in level. On a higher path, consumption per capita is always larger than on a lower one. A higher path represents a higher capital intensity (so long as capital intensity does not exceed its Golden Rule value) and a correspondingly higher propensity to save is required to maintain it.

An economy moving along one of these paths may "decide" to move to a higher one by lowering its propensity to consume. For a while, its growth rate will be higher, as the effects of increasing capital intensity and modernization are added to those of the underlying progress of technology. Eventually, however, capital intensity will cease to increase and the growth rate will converge to its natural value. The process can be repeated by further increases in the saving ratio, but the Golden Rule argument cited above sets a limit long before the propensity to consume reaches zero, indeed, when the propensity to save is equal to the elasticity of output with respect to capital accumulation. This is the highest path for consumption per capita.

Asymptotically, then, it appears that we have no choice about our *rate* of growth, but can choose only between parallel paths of different levels. But "asymptotically" is a very long time. The period of transition from one path to another, short from the perspective of the model-builder, may be measured

[3] See, for example, E. S. Phelps, "The New View of Investment: A Neoclassical Analysis," *Quarterly Journal of Economics*, November 1962, Vol. LXXVI, pp. 548–67.

in decades or generations. It is therefore not wholly misleading to regard society as choosing among growth *rates*.

Models of this kind take the rate of technological progress as exogenous. In fact, it is probably subject to improvement, like the degree of capital intensity, by expenditure of current resources. We still know very little about the technology that governs the production of applicable technological knowledge. What is required to keep the index of technology, which determines the productivity of labor and capital, growing at a constant exponential rate? Does it take simply a constant absolute amount of labor and capital? Does it take a constant fraction of the resources devoted to production? Does it take an input of resources growing at the same rate as the technology index itself? Only when we can answer such questions can we know whether and how the pace of economic growth is ultimately limited by the natural increase of the labor force.

A second reason for doubting that government measures can affect the intertemporal choices of society is the possibility that the private decisions of individuals can and will offset these measures. Suppose, for example, that the government levies new taxes and uses the proceeds for saving and investment, either through public expenditure, public lending to private investors, or through retirement of public debt. The government's purpose is to increase later consumption at the expense of earlier. But if this purpose is perfectly well understood, will not the public reduce its private saving in the knowledge that its collective saving is now doing part of the job?

I have two comments regarding this possibility. First, it may be that the government's saving corrects a situation of underinvestment, where public or private projects that would pay for themselves in social benefits (discounted at the time preference set of interest rates) were not being undertaken. In this case, the government's twist of the path will not be undone even if perfectly understood because the new path corresponds better to public preferences. Second, the assumption that the public correctly foresees all the consequences of government policy is farfetched. In the example above, economists would usually expect the new taxes to be paid in large part out of private consumption. Disposable income is reduced; and so, gradually, is the public's net financial claim on the government—a more tangible element in private balance sheets than the present value of future tax liabilities or of free services from government.

I conclude, therefore, that at least for the medium run, government can affect the growth of the economy; and I turn to the question whether it should.

III

In this section I propose to argue: (1) that government might legitimately have a growth policy, and indeed could scarcely avoid having one, even if private capital markets were perfect; (2) that capital markets are far from perfect and that private saving decisions are therefore based on an overconservative estimate of the social return to saving; and (3) that the terms on which even so advanced an economy as our own can trade present for future consumption seem to be very attractive.

1. *Government Neutrality in Intertemporal Choice.* Many economists and many other citizens will argue that the government should be neutral as between present and future. In their view, the capital markets produce an optimal result, balancing the time preferences of individuals, freely expressed through their consumption and saving behavior, against the technological opportunities for substituting consumption tomorrow for consumption today. Let us assume for the moment that government can be neutral in some meaningful sense and that the capital markets perform their assigned function. Even so, I believe government should have a growth policy, and only by accident a neutral one.

I fail to see why economists should advise the public that it is wrong for them collectively to supplement (or diminish) the provisions for the future they are making individually. I agree to the desirability of satisfying human preferences— that is what our kind of society and economy is all about. But I have never been able to understand why the preferences of individuals are worthy of respect *only* when they are expressed in the market, why the preferences of the very same individuals expressed politically should be regarded as distortions. Sometimes economists come close to rationalizing all market results and private institutions by the argument that they would not occur and survive if they were not optimally satisfying individuals' preferences. But political results and public institutions are not granted the benefit of presumptive justification-through-existence.

In both arenas, preferences certainly need to be guided by full and accurate information. In the arena of government policy, it is the business of economists to help the society know what it is doing, to understand the choices, benefits, costs, and risks it confronts, not simply to repeat *ad nauseam* that the best thing to do is nothing.

The case for explicit government policy in intertemporal social choice is especially strong. More than any other social institution, government represents the permanence and continuity of the society. And in a democracy, one way in which each generation uses government is to protect the interests of unborn generations against its own shortsighted and selfish instincts.

We cannot be sure that lineal family ties will give individuals sufficient motivation to provide for society's future. Suppose the individuals of a whole generation, deciding that their children and grandchildren might better start from scratch, were to proceed to consume their capital. Good capital markets might reflect this epidemic of acute time preference in a perfectly Pareto-optimal way. But would we as a nation feel that we were collectively discharging our obligations to our successors?

Through many activities of government, including conservation and public education, we have recognized a *generalized* obligation to equip the next generation—an obligation wholly distinct from our individual provisions for our own children. This generalized obligation acquires special force if we take seriously our ideals of equality of opportunity. We like to think that our society gives the members of each generation an equal chance in the race, or at least that their chances are not predetermined by family backgrounds. Besides requiring investment in human beings on a basis other than ability to pay, this ideal suggests redistributive taxation of estates. And if estate taxation dulls incentives to save for specific heirs, the government needs to replenish saving collectively.

But what is growth-neutral government finance anyway? I have already dismissed as farfetched one answer, namely, that any government finance is growth-neutral when it is fully and accurately foreseen, and accordingly offset, by taxpayers and by the beneficiaries of government services. Often a balanced budget is considered a growth-neutral fiscal policy. The budget in this rule is not, of course, the conventional U.S. administrative budget. Rather, the rule suggests that (a) net government investment should be covered by borrowing, with the Treasury competing in the capital markets with private investors for private saving, and that (b) other government expenditure, including allowance for consumption of public capital, should be covered by current taxes or fees.

The rule is clear-cut and has intuitive appeal. But it seems to bias social choice against the future when there is simply a shift in public preference from private consumption, present and future, to collective consumption, present and future. The rule would levy only enough new taxes to cover the additional collective consumption. But the evidence is that taxpayers would pay some of these new taxes from saving (especially if the collective consumption the taxes finance were of regrettable necessities like national defense rather than of services that clearly yield utility now and in future). Interest rates would rise and investment would be curtailed, even though no shift in social time preference has occurred. Clearly, the 10 percent of GNP which we have on average devoted to national defense in recent years has not come wholly from private or public consumption. True neutrality evidently would require a tighter fiscal policy the bigger the government's budget for current consumption.

But in any case, the quest for neutrality is probably a search for a will-o'-the-wisp. For it is not only the overall budget position of government, but also the specifics of taxation and expenditure which affect intertemporal choices. We have not yet learned how to implement the welfare economist's lump sum taxes. I have already given one example of a tax which is desirable in view of other social objectives but is bound to affect incentives for private accumulation of wealth. It will suffice to remind you also that our methods of taxation necessarily favor one kind of current consumption, leisure, both as against other current consumption and as against future consumption of products and leisure.

The major policy proposals of growthmen boil down to the suggestion that government should save—or save more—by making investments on its own account, subsidizing the investments of others, or by channeling tax money through the capital markets into private investment. This last item is the major purpose of the full-employment budget surplus for which Councils of Economic Advisers longed under both Presidents Eisenhower and Kennedy.

It is now widely recognized that in principle the government can match aggregate demand to the economy's capacity in a variety of ways. Its various instruments for regulating or stabilizing demand affect consumption and investment differently. A strong pro-growth policy would restrict consumption by taxation or by economy in government's current expenditure while stepping up public investment and encouraging private investment through tax incentives or low interest rates and high liquidity. The government cannot avoid choosing some combination of its demand-regulating instruments. Therefore government is bound to affect the composition of current output and society's provision for the future. Let us debate this choice of policy mixtures on its merits, weighing growth against its costs and against other objectives of policy, without encumbering the debate with a search for that combination which meets some elusive criterion of neutrality.

2. *Imperfections in Private Capital Markets.* I turn now to the second subject, the efficiency of the capital markets. Do private saving decisions reflect the real payoffs which nature and technology offer the economy? There are several reasons to believe that the answer is negative.

(a) *Monopoly and restrictions of entry.* The evidence is that the rates of return required of real investment projects by U.S. business corporations are very high—typically more than 10 percent after allowance for depreciation, obsolescence, and taxes. Rates of this magnitude are not only required *ex ante* but realized *ex post.* Why do these rates so greatly exceed the cost of borrowed funds, the earnings-to-price ratio of equity issues, and in general the rates of return available to savers?

One reason clearly is that the relevant markets are not purely competitive. A monopolistic or oligopolistic firm limits its expansion in product markets, its purchases in factor markets, and its calls on capital markets, because the firm takes into account that prices and rates in these markets will turn against it. The managers seek to maintain a market valuation of the firm in excess of the replacement cost of its assets, the differences representing the capitalized value of its monopoly power, often euphemistically called good will. Restrictions and costs of entry prevent other firms from competing this difference away. Foresighted and lucky investors receive the increases in the firm's market value in the form of capital gains. But the willingness of savers to value the assets of the firm above their cost, *i.e.,* to supply capital at a lower rate of return than the firm earns internally, is not translated into investment either by this firm or by others. One effect is to depress rates of return in more competitive sectors of the economy. But another result is to restrict total saving and investment.

(b) *Risks, private and social.* Risks provide a second reason for the observed divergence between the rates of return satisfactory to savers and those typically required of real investment projects. Some of these are risks to the economy as well as to the owners of the business: technological hazards, uncertainties about consumer acceptance of new products, or uncertainties about the future availability and social opportunity cost of needed factors of production. Even though these are social as well as private risks, it is not clear that society should take a risk-averse position toward them and charge a risk premium against those projects entailing more uncertainties than others. Presumably, society can pool such risks and realize with a very small margin of uncertainty the actuarial return on investments.

Moreover, some of the private risks are not social risks at all. Consider, for example, uncertainties about competition and market shares: if several rivals are introducing a new process or new product, the main uncertainties in the investment calculation of each are the future actions of the others. Consider, further, the high and sometimes prohibitive cost which many firms impute to external funds—apparently as insurance against loss of control to new shareowners, or, with extremely bad luck, to bondholders. If savers were offered the rates of return asked of and earned by business investments, in the form of assets that impose no more risk on the holder than is commensurate to the social risks involved, presumably they would choose to save more.

It is true, on the other hand, that some net saving is now motivated by personal contingencies that are likewise social risks of a much smaller order. But our society has created insuring institutions, both private and public, to reduce the need for oversaving to meet such contingencies. Except in the field of residential construction, it has created few similar institutions to prevent private risk-aversion from leading to underinvestment.

(c) *External returns to investment.* Some investments yield benefits which cannot be captured by the individual or firm making the initial outlay. Research and development expenditures and outlays for training of personnel are obvious cases in point. Government policy has already recognized this fact both in tax law and in government expenditures, and it is difficult to judge whether this recognition is sufficient. Kenneth Arrow[4] has pointed out that not only "R and D" but all forms of investment activity share in some degree the property that B may learn from A's doing. The support which this observation gives to a general policy of encouraging investment is somewhat tempered by reflecting that the same social process of "learning by doing" can occur in production of goods and services for current consumption. However, experience is most important as a teacher in new situations, and innovations are likely to require investment.

In regard to investment in human capacities and talents, it is by no means clear that public outlays are yet sufficient to reap the external benefits involved, or even that the relevant capital markets are sufficiently developed to permit individuals to earn the private benefits. I recognize that calculations of the rate of return to educational outlays depend critically on how much of these outlays are charged to current consumption. As an educator and ex-student, I am inclined to rate high the immediate utility-producing powers of education.

3. *The Payoff to Social Saving.* The burden of my remarks so far is that we cannot escape considering growth, or more precisely, intertemporal choice as an issue of public economic policy. We cannot assume either that the market settles the issue optimally or that government can be guided by some simple rules of neutrality. We—and here I mean the economics

---

[4] Kenneth Arrow, "The Economic Implications of Learning by Doing," *Review of Economic Studies*, June 1962, Vol. XXIX, pp. 155–73.

profession and the country—must confront head-on the question of whether the social payoff of faster growth in higher future consumption validates its cost in consumption foregone today. The issue that needs to be joined is typified by the contrast between Denison,[5] who estimates a very high investment requirement for a one-point increase in the medium-term growth rate (a ten-point increase in the ratio of current gross investment to GNP) and Solow,[6] who calculates a marginal investment requirement only about one-fifth as high.

Fortunately, the profession has now begun the task of computing rates of return on various kinds of investment, tangible and intangible. Thanks to theoretical advances in growth models and in handling the knotty problems of technological progress, vintage capital, and obsolescence, we have a better conceptual foundation for these tasks than we did only a few years ago. Phelps,[7] using the same conceptual approach as Solow,[8] has estimated the overall rate of return on tangible investment in the U.S. to be about 14 percent in 1954. And even this figure seems conservative in relation to some target rates of return of large industrial corporations reported by Lanzillotti.[9]

But whatever the true rates are, they must be compared with appropriate social rates of time preference. Here we may get some aid from the Golden Rule theory I have already cited.

Consider a family of exponential balanced-growth paths

[5] Edward F. Denison, *The Sources of Economic Growth in the United States and the Alternatives Before Us,* New York, Committee for Economic Development, 1962, Chap. 12.

[6] Robert M. Solow, "Technical Progress, Capital Formation, and Economic Growth," *American Economic Review,* May 1962, Vol. LII, pp. 76–86.

[7] See Phelps, note 3.

[8] Robert M. Solow, "Investment and Technical Progress," in K. J. Arrow, S. Karlin, and P. Suppes, eds., *Mathematical Methods in the Social Sciences 1959,* Stanford University Press, 1960, pp. 89–104.

[9] Robert F. Lanzillotti, "Pricing Objectives in Large Companies," *American Economic Review,* December 1958, Vol. XLVIII, pp. 921–40.

sharing a common growth rate; each member of the family has a constant saving ratio, and this ratio differs from path to path. It is also true that each path is characterized by a single technological interest rate, the same for all intervals of time. The theory of the Golden Rule tells us that the path of highest consumption per capita at every point in time is characterized by a gross saving ratio s equal to the elasticity of output with respect to capital α (this is also the share of nonlabor income in GNP if income distribution is governed by marginal productivity). Along the Golden Rule path, the social rate of interest is constant and equal to the rate of increase of the "effective" labor force. This, in turn, is equal to the natural rate of increase in the labor force plus the annual rate of improvement in labor quality due to technical progress.

If there is no technical improvement, consumption per capita remains constant over time; and along the Golden Rule path a dollar of per capita consumption saved today will produce a dollar, no more and no less, in per capita consumption tomorrow. The return on aggregate saving is just enough to keep up with population growth.

This rate of return represents impartiality between generations in this sense: When consumption per capita is the same tomorrow as today, there is no time preference; a dollar of consumption per capita is valued the same whenever it occurs.[10]

When there is technical progress, both the real wage and consumption per capita will advance at the annual rate at which labor quality improves, say λ. And along the Golden Rule path λ will also be the per annum rate of return, in future per capita consumption, on saving today. (A dollar of saving will yield in addition enough new capital to provide for the increment of population.) That is, an increase in per capita consumption of $1 at time t requires sacrifice of only $\$e^{-\lambda t}$ at time zero.

[10] See Koopmans, note 2.

It is reasonable to regard this rate of discount too as intertemporally impartial. Absence of time preference means that at *equal* consumption levels society values equally a dollar of future consumption and a dollar of present consumption. But on a path of *growing* per capita consumption, it is natural that a dollar of future consumption should no longer trade for current consumption at par. To take the rate of improvement in labor quality and in the real wage, λ, as the rate of time preference is to say in effect: Saving is justified if, and only if, it earns more than future consumers will gain anyway through the inexorable progress of technology. Thus, if the rate of technical progress is correctly foreseen, this principle meets a common criticism of growth, namely that there is no reason to save for future generations when technological progress will make them better off anyway. Figure 2 illustrates a social indifference curve between present and future per capita consumption such that there is no time preference

FIGURE 2

Suggested Criterion of Intertemporal Impartiality

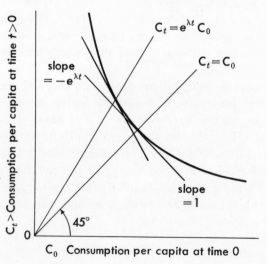

when the two are equal, but elsewhere a marginal rate of substitution that exceeds one in the same proportion that future consumption exceeds current consumption.

An economy saving at a constant rate s lower than α, the share of capital income in GNP, will be below its Golden Rule path. Its rate of return on saving will be accordingly higher than the Golden Rule rate. Indeed, the present value of the stream of returns from $1 of investment, computed at the Golden Rule rate on the theory that this is an appropriate impartial discount factor free of the taint of time preference, is equal to α/s. In the United States today, the ration α/s must exceed 1.5 and may be as high as 2.

For some models it is possible to compute the technological interest rate characteristic of a path with α/s greater than one, *i.e.*, of a path below the Golden Rule path. This is, in effect, what Phelps did to arrive at his estimates of the return on investment in the United States, cited above. Consider a model based on a Cobb-Douglas production function with variable factor proportions both *ex ante* and *ex post*. Let capital elasticity be α and labor elasticity $1 - \alpha$; the natural rate of increase in labor force n; constant technical progress expressed as improvement in the quality of labor at rate λ; a gross saving ratio s; depreciation of capital at a constant rate δ. The members of this family of growth paths share a rate of growth $n + \lambda$ in aggregate output, investment, and consumption, and a rate of growth λ in the real wage and in per capita consumption. The rate of interest characteristic of a path is different depending whether technical progress is assumed to be (a) disembodied and affecting all capital old or new, or (b) embodied in new vintage capital only. The expressions for the rate of interest in the two cases are as follows (for their derivation see Appendix below):

a) disembodied technical progress

$$r = \frac{\alpha}{s}(n + \lambda + \delta) - \delta$$

b) embodied technical progress

$$r = \frac{\alpha}{s}(n + \lambda + \delta) - \delta + \frac{\lambda(1 - \alpha)}{s} - \frac{\lambda(1 - \alpha)}{\alpha}$$

If, for example, $n = .015$, $\lambda = .03$, $\delta = .03$, and $s = .20$, then $r = .095$ in case (a) and $r = .135$ in case (b). The difference reflects the fact, originally emphasized by Solow,[11] that additional saving moves the economy toward a higher path faster in the vintage-capital model and therefore is rewarded sooner with higher consumption.

The evidence is uncertain, and there is a clear need for more refined and reliable estimates of the parameters on which the issue turns. I believe the evidence suggests that policy to accelerate growth, to move the economy to a higher path, would pay. That is, the returns to a higher saving and investment ratio would be positive, if evaluated by a reasonable set of social time preference interest rates. This seems to me the strongest reason for advocating growth policy.

APPENDIX

1. Let $I(v)$ be gross investment at time (vintage) v, and let $\rho(v, t)$ be its marginal productivity at time t. Then the present value of the stream of returns from investment of one dollar at time v is

$$\int_v^\infty e^{-\int_v^t r(u)du} \rho(v, t)dt$$

Setting this present value equal to 1 for all v defines the series $r(u)$ of instantaneous technological interest rates.

In the models under discussion in the text, calendar time does not affect $\rho(v, t)$, which can therefore be written as $\rho(t - v)$. It follows that $r(u)$ is a constant, and we may find it from:

---

[11] See Solow, note 8.

(1) $$\int_0^\infty e^{-r(t-v)} \rho(t - v) \, d(t - v) = 1$$

The gross income to capital at time t, if capital of each vintage is paid its marginal product, is

$$\alpha Q(t) = \int_{-\infty}^t I(v) \, \rho(v, t) \, dv = \int_0^\infty I(t - v) \, \rho(t - v) \, d(t - v)$$

where $Q(t)$ is gross output summed over all vintages, and α is capital's share. Now if investment is growing exponentially at rate g—the rate of growth of output—then $I(t - v) = I(t)e^{-g(t-v)}$.

Therefore:

(2) $$\frac{\alpha Q(t)}{I(t)} = \frac{\alpha}{s} = \int_0^\infty e^{-g(t-v)} \rho(t - v) \, d(t - v)$$

where s is the saving ratio, constant along the path. The right-hand side will be recognized as the present value of the stream of returns from investment when the discount factor is g rather than r. This present value exceeds 1 whenever α/s exceeds 1.

2. The above argument shows that $r \gtreqless g$ as $\alpha \gtreqless s$. It remains to derive the explicit expressions for r given in the text.

(a) Disembodied progress:

Let $Q(v, t)$ be the output and $L(v, t)$ the labor input associated with capital made at time v.

(3) $$Q(v, t) = A(I(v) \, e^{-\delta(t-v)})^\alpha (L(v, t)e^{\lambda t})^{1-\alpha}$$

The marginal product of capital:

(4) $$\rho(v, t) = \alpha \, \frac{Q(v, t)}{I(v)} = A\alpha e^{-\alpha\delta(t-v)} \, e^{\lambda(1-\alpha)t} \left(\frac{L(v, t)}{I(v)} \right)^{1-\alpha}$$

The marginal product of labor:

(5)

$$w(t) = (1 - \alpha) \, \frac{Q(v, t)}{L(v, t)} = A(1 - \alpha)e^{-\alpha\delta(t-v)}e^{\lambda(1-\alpha)t} \left(\frac{L(v, t)}{I(v)} \right)^{-\alpha}$$

$$w(t)^{-\frac{(1-\alpha)}{\alpha}} =$$

$$A^{-\frac{(1-\alpha)}{\alpha}} (1 - \alpha)^{-\frac{(1-\alpha)}{\alpha}} e^{(1-\alpha)\delta(t-v)} e^{-\lambda \frac{(1-\alpha)^2}{\alpha} t} \left(\frac{L(v,t)}{I(v)}\right)^{1-\alpha}$$

$$\rho(v,t) = A^{\frac{1}{\alpha}} \alpha (1-\alpha)^{+\frac{(1-\alpha)}{\alpha}} e^{-\delta(t-v)} e^{\frac{(1-\alpha)}{\alpha} \lambda t} w(t)^{-\left(\frac{(1-\alpha)}{\alpha}\right)}$$

Since the real wage w grows at rate λ,

$$\rho(v,t) = A^{\frac{1}{\alpha}} \alpha (1-\alpha)^{\frac{(1-\alpha)}{\alpha}} e^{-\delta(t-v)} e^{\frac{(1-\alpha)}{\alpha} \lambda t} (w(0)e^{\lambda t})^{-\left(\frac{1-\alpha}{\alpha}\right)}$$

$$\rho(v,t) = A^{\frac{1}{\alpha}} \alpha (1-\alpha)^{\frac{1-\alpha}{\alpha}} e^{-\delta(t-v)} w(0)^{-\left(\frac{1-\alpha}{\alpha}\right)}$$

Thus $\rho(v,t)$ can be written as $\rho(t-v)$ and indeed

$$(6) \qquad \rho(v,t) = \rho(t-v) = \rho(v,v) e^{-\delta(t-v)} = \rho(0) e^{-\delta(t-v)}$$

To find r we set $\int_0^\infty e^{-r(t-v)} \rho(t-v) \, d(t-v) = 1$

Therefore:

$$(7) \qquad \rho(0) \int_0^\infty e^{-r(t-v)} e^{-\delta(t-v)} \, d(t-v) = 1$$

and $r = \rho(0) - \delta$

From section 1 we know:

$$\rho(0) \int_0^\infty e^{-g(t-v)} e^{-\delta(t-v)} \, d(t-v) = \frac{\alpha}{s}$$

Therefore:

$$(8) \qquad\qquad \rho(0) = \frac{\alpha}{s} (g + \delta)$$

Since $g = n + \lambda$ we have:

$$(9) \qquad\qquad r = \frac{\alpha}{s} (n + \lambda + \delta) - \delta$$

(b) Embodied progress:

In this case:

$$(10) \qquad Q(v,t) = A(I(v) e^{-\delta(t-v)})^\alpha (L(v,t) e^{\lambda v})^{1-\alpha}$$

By reasoning similar to (a) we obtain:

$$\rho(v,\, t) = A^{\frac{1}{\alpha}} \alpha (1 - \alpha)^{\frac{1-\alpha}{\alpha}} e^{-\delta(t-v)} e^{\frac{(1-\alpha)}{\alpha} \lambda v} w(t)^{-\left(\frac{1-\alpha}{\alpha}\right)}$$

$$(11) \quad \rho(v,\, t) = A^{\frac{1}{\alpha}} \alpha (1 - \alpha)^{\frac{1-\alpha}{\alpha}} e^{\left(-\delta - \frac{(1-\alpha)\lambda}{\alpha}\right)(t-v)} w(0)^{-\left(\frac{1-\alpha}{\alpha}\right)}$$

Once again $\rho(v,\, t)$ can be written as $\rho(t - v)$, and

$$\rho(t - v) = \rho(0) e^{-\left(\delta + \frac{(1-\alpha)\lambda}{\alpha}\right)(t-v)}$$

The same procedure used in (a) gives:

$$(12) \qquad\qquad r = \rho(0) - \delta - \frac{(1 - \alpha)\lambda}{\alpha}$$

and

$$(13) \qquad\quad \rho(0) = \frac{\alpha}{s}\left(g + \delta + \frac{(1 - \alpha)}{\alpha}\lambda\right)$$

$$= \frac{\alpha}{s}(n + \lambda + \delta) + \frac{(1 - \alpha)}{s}\lambda$$

Therefore:

$$(14) \quad r = \frac{\alpha}{s}(n + \lambda + \delta) - \delta + \left(\frac{1 - \alpha}{s}\right)\lambda - \left(\frac{1 - \alpha}{\alpha}\right)\lambda.$$

Part V

U.S. Economic Growth and World Leadership

BY

Richard N. Cooper

* This essay was written in early 1964, in the midst of recovery from
an economic recession and before extensive U.S. military involvement in
Vietnam. It has been modified only in the updating of a few figures, and
should be read accordingly.

Surprisingly, a recent symposium on "Freedoms and Restraints" in American foreign policy does not mention the state of the domestic economy—its level of employment and output, its distribution of income, and its rate of economic growth—as an important factor in shaping our foreign policy or foreign reaction to it. And an earlier symposium considered the "instruments" of the United States in achieving international stability and progress without numbering domestic economic policies for growth among them.[1] Can it be that economic growth in the United States has no bearing on the U.S. position of world leadership? Or is the bearing so insignificant that it can be neglected? Or do such views constitute one more instance of the false separation between domestic and international considerations that American observers so often make?

In this volume, other essays suggest that the rate of economic growth can—and should—be raised as a matter of public policy. One reason why it should is that the rate of economic growth at home will influence considerably the success of the United States in achieving its objectives of foreign policy. Domestic growth is an "instrument" of foreign policy: A high rate of growth will provide additional freedoms, and a low one added restraints, in pursuit of our international aims.

[1] "American Foreign Policy—Freedoms and Restraints," *Daedalus*, Fall 1962; and *International Stability and Progress*, The American Assembly, 1957.

Economic growth can influence foreign policy in three broad ways: It can increase the total amount of resources available for pursuit of our foreign policy objectives in the future. It can change the size and rate of growth of our markets for the products of the world's less developed areas. Finally, it can shape the "image" which the United States projects to the world—and to itself—in the ideological conflict of the cold war. Each of these facets will be discussed in turn. In a concluding section I shall consider whether heavy U.S. commitments abroad and the present weakness in the international payments position of the United States will hinder the achievement of more rapid economic growth.

I. RESOURCES AVAILABLE FOR INTERNATIONAL OBJECTIVES

Growth is the "great reconciler" among competing claims on output. Our affluent society has not yet provided a cornucopia of goods and services fully satisfying all our needs, public and private, foreign and domestic. Resources are still scarce, and output must be rationed among competing objectives and desires. By adding one more claimant to today's output—investment in human resources and knowledge and in material capital—we ease the problem of satisfying tomorrow's needs.

The Federal Government is charged by the Constitution with shaping and executing our foreign policy. To do so effectively requires large resources, especially in the areas of defense spending and foreign aid. More rapid economic growth would ease the task of supplying resources to both without requiring tax rates that would inhibit incentives to work. If output and incomes grow rapidly, government tax *revenues* increase correspondingly even at lower tax *rates*.

A. *Military Expenditures.* The military position of the United States clearly influences its foreign policy. America's military pre-eminence catapulted it to a position of world leadership during and immediately after World War II and has preserved that position down to the present. An erosion of that position beyond a certain point would erode U.S. influence abroad—influence which, if properly used, can guide foreign effort and ingenuity toward those objectives the United States regards as desirable.

Defense spending can influence foreign policy quite directly. Clearly the protective presence of U.S. troops in Europe has made Germany a useful U.S. ally on many postwar issues and provided a sense of security which helped foster rapid European growth. Conversely, our unilateral abandonment of the Skybolt missile in late 1962, whatever the merits of the decision on military grounds, surprised and irritated the United Kingdom—and we had to make up for it with a bilateral agreement at Nassau in December 1962. This in turn is said to have precipitated de Gaulle's rejection of Britain's entry into the European Economic Community—thereby thwarting, at least temporarily, a major objective of U.S. policy.

We usually think of the military budget as the one area, apart from the annual rivers and harbors bill, which is immune to drastic budget-cutting. Indeed, the Congress has on more than one occasion appropriated more for military expenditures than the President has requested. Yet despite this relative immunity, military costs are frequently cut. Under the pressure of a low-budget ceiling, decisions are often made to cut out the "frills," the extra margin of precision or effectiveness which seems to be too costly relative to the expected benefits. Reduction of real waste and inefficiency is of course desirable in defense expenditures as elsewhere. But, "economizing" in military spending, as elsewhere in government, often also involves decisions not to take up new programs which are widely accepted as desirable, to stretch out the use of dated equipment one more year, to accept a slightly inferior product because of its lower cost.

The U.S. Navy in 1963 extended the replacement schedule

for old World War II aircraft carriers still under commission; and it will not get expensive nuclear power for its new carriers.[2] Both decisions were governed by budgetary limitations. The TFX aircraft controversy of 1962 arose because of both short- and long-range budgetary limitations. A single plane could approximate the functions of two separate planes, one for the Air Force and one for the Navy, at considerably lower total development and procurement costs. And a single model would permit future savings on inventories of spare parts. But the plane admittedly represented a compromise between the functional requirements of the Navy and the Air Force.

Decisions such as these that weaken our military position, even marginally, can weaken our foreign policy. More rapid growth in the United States will not eliminate the need to eliminate marginal programs because of budgetary constraints; there will always be some expenditures which do not seem worth the cost. But the margin will be further out; expenditures which we feel unable to afford now would be acceptable with more rapid growth. There has been some talk about our ability to cut defense spending by up to one-quarter without impairing national security. If true, this gain in efficiency should be highly applauded; that will itself provide a wider budgetary margin. More rapid growth is analogous to *continuous* improvements in efficiency over time, providing an ever greater margin for safety.

B. *Foreign Assistance.* Unlike military expenditures, our foreign aid program is not immune to drastic budget-cutting; indeed the entire program seems to some citizens to be a mere frill. The country witnessed a sharp cut of $1.5 billion in the foreign assistance program of $4.5 billion proposed by President Kennedy for fiscal year 1964, and further cuts in appropriations not related to Vietnam have been made since then. This cut was made even though the proposed program

[2] Since this was written, a contract has been awarded to design a second nuclear-powered aircraft carrier.

had been represented as the "rock bottom" requirement with many "marginal" projects already shed under the pressure of public criticism.

Giving foreign assistance to low-income nations is a complicated process. We have no clear idea of how much development aid is needed to give economic growth abroad a decisive boost. We do not even know whether such a boost can be given. We do know, however, that throughout the less-developed areas of the world there is a dearth of capital. Especially lacking is "infrastructure" or social overhead capital for transportation and communications, water and power. We know that there is an equally retarding lack of technical knowledge and skills. Finally, we know that both capital and skills must increase substantially before incomes can be raised significantly above the levels of poverty which now prevail.

I take for granted that raising per capita income above these subsistence levels is a desirable objective for U.S. policy. Fifty or even thirty years ago one could have made a case— though not a very appealing one—that U.S. interests would best be served by "letting sleeping dogs lie." While it was regrettable on humanitarian grounds, the poverty-stricken and disease-ridden three-fourths of the world was politically inert and militarily effete; it could not threaten the more fortunate and more progressive white domains of Europe, North America, and Oceania. Such arguments no longer have force. The leaders of the poor countries have become self-conscious about their poverty and their inertia. They are painfully aware of their anachronistic position in a world where man is able to harness as much nonhuman energy in a year as has been used in all previous human history, and quite possibly able to visit other planets before the century is over. These leaders are determined, by one means or another, to improve their countries' status in the world; first, by eliminating political subjugation through gaining national independence and, second, by raising their capacity to feed, house, clothe, defend, and educate their growing populations through economic growth. They increasingly echo the late President Kennedy's assertion that "political independence is but a mockery without economic advancement."

The determination by leaders in the "awakening" nations to pursue economic development at whatever cost puts the United States, as the leading nation in the non-communist world, in the sometimes awkward position both of providing a model for economic development and of being expected to help materially the new nations get their development started. The United States is in this position whether Americans like it or not. If the United States fails to provide guidance and assistance, many less developed countries have the option of turning to the Soviet bloc for both. The Soviet Union, of course, does not represent an unlimited source of foreign assistance; on the contrary, its productive capacity is at present under heavy strain from existing claims on output, and it too is showing some reluctance to expand foreign aid. But continuing rapid growth in the Soviet Union will make possible additional foreign assistance, which will be extended if it is expected to lead to high political and strategic gains. The more ardent Soviet expansionists are unlikely to have forgotten Lenin's dictum that the route to Paris and Berlin is via Calcutta.

The principal rationale for U.S. economic assistance is that it enhances the security of the United States and, indeed, the system of Western values. It is often said to do so by minimizing the probability of "social revolution." This argument is very doubtful. Foreign aid as such is not likely to minimize change, even if minimizing change were desirable. Rather, foreign aid can be used to influence the direction of change, and in particular to bolster those internal elements favorable toward Western ideals and toward the United States. For although economic growth as an objective is clearly compatible with fundamental principles of Western civilization, and is indeed a prerequisite for their full realization, growth can also be pursued effectively in total disregard of these principles. Where political power is in the hands of individuals less devoted to Western values than to raising national incomes, we cannot be confident that the values will take root. Foreign assistance now equals about 25 percent of total fixed capital formation in the less-developed countries of the free world. Without this assistance, growth-minded leaders might be strongly tempted by the Soviet example, now followed so ruthlessly in China, of extracting resources for investment by forcibly reducing consumption below already abysmal levels.

We do not yet have well-developed criteria for extending foreign assistance with maximum efficiency in achieving these objectives. Ideally these criteria would be geared to the capital or foreign exchange requirements of the less-developed countries themselves. But since economists know little about measuring the external benefits (which many believe to be large) attending investment in men and productive capacity in the early stages of development, a project-by-project examination of investment possibilities in the less-developed countries would seriously understate the amount of assistance which could be fruitfully given. It is on this assumption that the United States and other donor nations have supported the United Nations' objective that 1 percent of the donor countries' combined national income should be extended as foreign assistance.

It is of course true that too much foreign assistance, given prematurely and inefficiently, can discredit the United States and do violence to our objectives. This should be avoided. But when foreign aid can serve our broad aims, the resources should be made available. A more rapid rate of economic growth will enable the United States to meet the 1 percent target more easily without requiring reductions in expenditures elsewhere; and it would increase the absolute amount of assistance more rapidly over time once the 1 percent target was reached.

II. EXPORT GROWTH FOR THE DEVELOPING NATIONS

Foreign assistance is only one way, and not always the best way, to assist economic growth in the poor parts of the world. Raising exports is for many countries a more efficient way to stimulate investment, provide employment, and raise incomes. Like foreign assistance, exports provide foreign exchange for the purchase of needed imports. In addition, exports provide outlets for production. Growing export markets increase profit-making opportunities where they are altogether too rare, encourage private investment, and stimulate private entrepreneurial activity. One of the most severe obstacles to economic growth in the developing nations is the absence of obvious socially productive, profit-making opportunities. This obstacle can be partially removed through investment in social overhead capital and in education, and foreign assistance can play an important role in providing both. But large and growing markets are also essential to the development process, particularly if private enterprise is to play an important role in it. Markets overseas, especially for manufactured products, can in part make up for domestic demand where the latter is insufficient to permit economies of large-scale production and distribution.

In an economy as self-contained as the United States, a rapid growth in productive capacity corresponds at full employment to a rapid growth in output and incomes. Raising incomes and output in the United States would help raise export earnings of the less-developed countries in two respects. First, there would be higher demand for imports into the United States, particularly imports of raw materials to supply growing production. Second, a fully employed, rapidly growing economy would ease adjustment to increased competition from abroad and would thus reduce the demands for protection against growing imports, particularly imports of manufactured products, from the less-developed countries.

A. *Rising Demand for Primary Products.* Export earnings accounted for about $26 billion in foreign exchange receipts of the less developed countries from the industrialized countries in 1963, compared with $6 billion for foreign assistance and $3 billion for private long-term investment. Export earnings thus provide the major source of foreign exchange for needed imports and for servicing debt to the developed countries. Growing disenchantment with foreign aid as a tool of economic policy increases further the future importance of export earnings. Yet at a time when both import needs and foreign debt have both been growing rapidly, the export earnings of the less-developed countries have risen only modestly. Between 1953 and 1962 their total export earnings grew only $8 billion, or 38 percent, compared with a growth in total world exports of $63 billion, or 81 percent. This overall increase in export earnings of course obscures a great diversity of experience among the less-developed countries, with some countries, such as Iraq, Israel, Mexico, Taiwan, and Venezuela, enjoying a sharp increase in earnings, and others, such as Brazil, Colombia, and Indonesia, actually experiencing an absolute decline in earnings.

The poor record of export earnings can be explained in part by falling export prices: according to the United Nations index, export prices of food and raw materials (which account for 85 percent of all exports from the less-developed countries) fell 12 percent from 1953 to 1962, thus reducing the earnings on a rising volume of exports. This decline in export prices cost the less-developed countries more than $3 billion in foreign exchange (on the assumption that the increase in export volume was not stimulated by the price reductions), which is nearly as much as the total increase in foreign assistance during the period.[3]

[3] Since this was written exports of the less-developed countries have fared very much better. Their export earnings grew from $23 billion in

The export position of the less-developed countries is somewhat worse than this combination of lagging growth and sagging prices implies. The American economy was sluggish after 1957, but Western Europe and Japan experienced spectacular economic growth during the fifties, and this difference in growth was reflected in imports. While U.S. imports from the less-developed countries grew only 12 percent ($700 million) in the period 1953–62, imports into Western Europe grew 47 percent ($3.8 billion) and those of Japan grew 75 percent ($700 million). However, growth in Western Europe, while still high, is likely to be somewhat slower in the late sixties than it was in the fifties and early sixties. The Commission of the European Economic Community projected annual growth in real Gross National Product (GNP) of the six Common Market countries at 4.5 percent a year from 1960 to 1970, compared with 5.6 percent during the period 1953–60. Moreover, the trade preference accorded to the former African colonies of France and Belgium in the Common Market will reduce the earnings of other less-developed countries, and inauguration of a common agricultural policy will also sharply limit some markets.

Higher U.S. growth would not only increase the volume of U.S. imports from the less-developed countries; it would also tend to buoy up the prices of the primary products on which they rely so heavily for foreign exchange. This upward pressure on prices would boost export earnings from the much larger exports of primary products to Europe and Japan, assuming that firmer prices do not substantially reduce the level of demand.

In a recent study of the trade problems of less-developed areas, Bela Balassa has estimated that a one-half percentage point increase in the growth rate of all industrial countries would raise the projected imports from the less-developed

---

1962 to nearly $31 billion in 1966, a rise of 44 percent. Nearly $1 billion of this increase was due to higher prices for primary products. Foreign aid and private capital flows also increased, though not so strikingly.

countries by over $3 billion in 1975, from $33.1 billion to $36.2 billion.[4]

Enlarged export markets in the industrial countries of the West would reduce the temptation, very strong in less-developed countries with excess capacity in primary products, to trade with the Soviet bloc. Partly for political reasons, partly because growing production has enlarged its need to seek essential industrial materials beyond its own borders, the Soviet Union has in recent years increased sharply its imports from the less-developed countries. It has inaugurated a number of "prospecting" ventures in search for new sources of supply, holding out the promise of greatly increased export earnings to such countries as Afghanistan, Ethiopia, Ghana, Mali, and Pakistan. Growing Soviet imports from the non-communist world is a natural development, and sales to the Soviet Union can be as useful a source of foreign exchange as sales to the industrial West. But such sales should not have to be made by nations in desperate search for markets and under circumstances which place the Soviet Union in the role of generous benefactor rather than needy buyer. A more rapid growth of markets in the West will permit the less-developed countries to choose their trading partners with greater circumspection.

B. *Reduced Protection Against Manufactured Imports.* Full employment and more rapid economic growth in the United States will improve the exporting prospects of the less-developed countries in still another way: by reducing the clamor for protection against growing imports of goods traditionally produced at home. Expanding markets in the United States and elsewhere will have the additional advantage of reducing the even greater clamor for protection in the less-developed countries themselves.

It is difficult to escape the fact that production and exports

[4] Bela Balassa, *Trade Prospects for Developing Countries,* Homewood, Ill.: Richard D. Irwin, for the Yale Economic Growth Center, 1964, Table A3.1.2, p. 390.

from the developing countries will shift increasingly toward simple manufactures which compete directly with products hitherto made primarily in the industrial countries. Apart from petroleum, exports of manufactures from the less-developed countries have risen more rapidly than any other commodity group, and they are certain to grow rapidly in the future. Yet such exports often threaten employment and profits in some industries in the importing countries. The most widely cited example is textiles, but the less-developed countries are already exporting iron and steel products, rubber manufactures, hard board, and other manufactures in increasing quantity.

The protectionist response in the United States can be seen in the case of textiles, where imports still supply less than 5 percent of total consumption but have become substantial enough in certain lines to alarm both labor and management. In Britain, traditionally the major exporter of textiles, imports now equal nearly two-thirds of textile exports. The international Long-term Cotton Textile Agreement of 1962 is a protectionist device to limit the growth of textile imports into the industrial countries. It was designed to provide for some growth in textile imports but at the same time to prevent "market disruption." It should be clear that this objective is achieved at the expense of potentially much greater increases in cotton textile exports, hence export earnings, from the less-developed countries, although in reality the Agreement undoubtedly reduced pressures for even more restrictive measures to limit imports.

Calls for protection can take other, more damaging forms. Applications for escape-clause action under the Trade Agreements Act rose sharply in the period 1957–62, and many of the offending imports came from Japan, which in many ways presages the changing composition of exports as a country develops. Moreover, the Act for International Development of 1961 requires that no development loans be made to any foreign enterprise which could compete with U.S. production unless the recipient country agrees that during the life of the loan no more than 20 percent of the enterprise's output will be exported to the United States. Yet profitable, growing export industries are precisely what the less-developed countries need, and it is in such industries that investment and growth should take place.

There has been talk of extending the principle of "controlled market entry" embodied in the Long-term Cotton Textile Agreement to other products. Far preferable would be to maintain full employment with a rapid rate of growth. When unemployment is low and demand is pressing against capacity, workers and businessmen displaced by imports can shift to alternative forms of employment much more easily. When jobs are plentiful, workers will be far less inclined to demand import restrictions. Adjustment assistance for retraining and relocation, such as that provided for in the Trade Expansion Act of 1962, can then operate most effectively.

Similarly, when the total market is rising rapidly, the likelihood of *absolute* declines in production due to increased import competition is lessened. Growth in industries competing with imports will be stunted by rising imports, but production and employment may not actually fall. Thus in an environment of rapid growth, already-existing interests will experience much less hardship as a result of the relative alterations that rising imports bring about in the composition of output. This has been the experience of the members of the European Economic Community since its founding in 1957. Problems of adjustment have been far less than anticipated, the schedule for eliminating internal trade barriers has consequently been rapidly accelerated, and the Social Fund set up to assist readjustment remains virtually unused.

Expanding export markets will also reduce protectionist tendencies in the less-developed countries. New theories of restrictive commercial policy are being devised, and old ones are being revived. These are fortified by disappointing gains in export earnings. While a certain amount of protection may be desirable and even necessary for getting efficient industries started—indeed, the less-developed countries look to our own history going back to Hamilton's Report on Manufactures for support—the indiscriminate restriction of trade is in the interests of neither the United States nor the less-developed countries themselves.

III. THE WORLD "IMAGE" OF THE UNITED STATES

We come finally to the question which several years ago figured most prominently in popular discussion about U.S. growth, namely, the "growth race" with the U.S.S.R. But this should be put in a broader context of the "image" of the United States abroad—and American self-respect at home.

The psychological impact of U.S. growth is necessarily intangible and more difficult to evaluate than the impact of growth on expenditures for national security or on the export earnings of the less-developed countries. It is also well outside the area where an economist can safely tread. But it is nonetheless important.

In his speech to the Twentieth Party Congress in 1956, Khrushchev argued that "the great advantages of the socialist economic system, the high rate of development of social production, enable us to carry out in an historically very brief period the main economic task of the U.S.S.R.—to catch up and surpass the most developed capitalist countries in per capita output." Soviet leaders have been plying the same theme ever since then, and hope someday to "bury capitalism" under a pile of Soviet-made goods. A challenge need not be accepted merely because it is offered; and when there is no interested audience it can be graciously ignored. But Khrushchev's challenge to the industrial West does have two interested audiences: the people of the Soviet bloc and the vast population of the less-developed areas. Many young leaders in the less-developed countries are vitally interested in economic growth and are in search of a "model." Few of them look to the United States for such a model—the circumstances of our own growth from infancy were too different, too prolonged, and too uncoordinated. But some are tempted to duplicate Soviet techniques, while others are inclined more toward a path of development which allows greater scope for private initiative and individual freedom.

We should not suppose that these choices will be uninfluenced by the relative performance of the United States and the Soviet Union. Some difference in growth rates can be rationalized. The U.S.S.R. is a "younger" economy, further behind in technology and in scale of production, and therefore able to "catch up" by sacrificing current consumption for greater future output. Moreover, the great human cost of Soviet growth during the Stalinist era is too high even for the leaders of many countries where human lives are cheap. On the other hand, the lackluster performance of the United States in the late 1950's cannot be easily dismissed. During the fifties, real GNP in the United States grew less than 3.5 percent annually compared with an estimated 7 percent for Soviet Russia. The United Nations Secretariat has estimated that industrial production in the Soviet Union and Eastern Europe accounted for 29 percent of the world total in 1965, compared with 33 percent for the United States and Canada.[5]

Isaac Deutscher, the Soviet specialist, has stated that "the outcome of the industrial contest between the U.S.S.R. and the U.S.A. will indeed have a decisive influence on the ideological conflict of our age."[6] He argues that an economically poor Soviet Russia had nothing to offer other countries—nothing to compensate for its admitted lack of freedoms. The

[5] At prices of 1958. Computed from the U.N. *Monthly Bulletin of Statistics.* The United Nations estimates, in this difficult area of international comparisons, are not above criticism; in particular, Soviet industrial production may be overstated because the official exchange rate was used to convert Soviet rubles to dollars.

[6] *The Great Contest,* New York: Oxford University Press, 1960, p. 94.

contrast between the Marshall Plan of the U.S. and the stiff reparations payments required by the U.S.S.R. following World War II made a very strong impression in Europe. Communism lost out there, and continues to lose, partly because of the contrast in living standards, for example, between East and West Germany. Pressures have even mounted in Eastern Europe to shift toward Western economic ways. But Russia's growth from an underdeveloped country to the world's second industrial power in one generation has not failed to impress many leaders in the less-developed countries. Marxism holds that capitalism must collapse because of its own internal contradictions. The more factually minded Marxists must now concede that capitalism has somehow adapted itself to avoid the self-generated collapse. Such Marxists are now shifting their argument: While capitalism can survive, they say, it is inherently less efficient than socialism and cannot match either the spiritual or the material achievements of a socialist system.

In every developing country there are exponents of a variety of approaches to development, and the persuasiveness of each approach depends in part on the examples that can be cited for and against it. In the internal debates we must assume take place, the position of those favoring the Soviet approach will be strengthened by a weak relative performance of the United States. Moreover, U.S. performance will influence the debates *whether or not* Americans explicitly accept the Soviet challenge—there is, in this sense, no way to reject the challenge. Good U.S. performance provides good debating material for those friendly to the United States and to Western values. And since the less-developed areas are not likely to be as inconsequential in their influence on world affairs in the next century as they were in the century past, "winning the debate" in these countries can be of great importance for the West and for Western values.

The United States is of course not alone in providing an example of a vigorous, rapidly growing, free enterprise economy. The economic performance in Western Europe and

Japan during the past decade has demonstrated that a communist government and Soviet-style planning are not necessary to achieve growth rates in excess of 5 percent—and even 10 percent—annually. But the United States remains the leading nation of the West, and excellent performance elsewhere cannot altogether compensate for poor performance here.

Moreover, the United States must concern itself with its "image" in the other industrial countries at least as much as in the less developed areas. Economic growth is perhaps less important in this respect than full employment and equilibrium in the balance of payments. But U.S. dealings with de Gaulle have not been helped by Americans, private and official, parading to Paris several years ago to find the "secret" of French economic growth. It is no doubt very flattering, but some are unmoved by flattery. The strong economic performance of France, and the relatively weak performance of the Anglo-Saxon countries, undoubtedly increased European receptivity to the "dirigist" economic policies urged by France on the European Common Market.

Finally, there is America's image of itself. Americans are raised to believe that the United States has the best, the most, and the biggest of everything, and a discouraging number persist in this belief well into adulthood. A transformation of this view to something closer to reality would doubtless be desirable, but it is a transformation which should take place gradually and by accumulating evidence from other peoples friendly to Americans, not by startling achievements by the countries believed to be most antagonistic to the United States. Gunnar Myrdal, the Swedish economist and sociologist, has observed that Americans are magnanimous and broad-minded winners but very poor losers. A steady erosion of U.S. economic, technological, and scientific leadership by a rapid Soviet economic growth and the added freedom such growth permits, for example, to get to the moon or to woo successfully the less-developed countries with timely and well-placed foreign assistance, will only create a sense of frustration in a United States which cannot point to similar achievements. Such frustration may vent itself in the adoption of attitudes or policies which are inimical to the long-run interests both of the United States and of the rest of the free world. Peoples and governments are still moved by national pride. Sometimes hurt pride may galvanize this country to action, as it seemed to after the first Sputnik in 1957; but at other times it may only fortify a national paranoia that produces witch-hunts at home and stultifies foreign policy, as in the case of China and Cuba, to a point at which it becomes incapable of adapting imaginatively to changing circumstances.

IV. EXTERNAL CONSTRAINTS ON U.S. GROWTH

It should be clear from the discussion above that a strong and rapidly growing U.S. economy can strengthen the U.S. position in dealing with our allies and antagonists abroad. But what about the negative side of the ledger? Some may be tempted to argue that we should grow more slowly, not more rapidly, for rapid growth will make it all the more difficult for developing countries to reduce the income gap, a reduction which is necessary if nations are to coexist peacefully and cooperatively. On this argument, rapid U.S. growth may do positive harm, by raising the aspirations of the world's poor much more rapidly than the growth in productivity can satisfy them. If that is so, the outlook for peaceful international co-operation is bleak indeed. The income differentials existing between the United States and the less-developed countries are already so large that they will continue to increase even if the less-developed countries grow much more rapidly than the United States.[7]

[7] To take an extreme possibility for purposes of illustration, growth in per capita income in the United States at only 1 percent a year

Fortunately perhaps, the differential is so large that small changes in the income gap will not be perceptible. Most development planning in less-developed countries rightly focuses on internal growth objectives rather than global income distribution. What is important is a sense of progress relative to one's own recent past, not relative to Western Europe or the United States.

A second and more persuasive possible entry on the negative side of the ledger is that rapid growth will aggravate the already weak U.S. balance of payments position and thereby worsen the favorable "image" which growth is designed to produce. Indeed, some of the benefits from growth alleged above result precisely from the rise in imports which faster growth can be expected to generate.[8]

Since 1958 the United States has run unexpectedly large deficits in its international payments. Because U.S. gold reserves and lines of credit with the surplus countries (largely those of continental Europe) are limited, such large deficits cannot be financed indefinitely. They have already forced the U.S. government to a number of expedients to reduce the deficit and to finance the remaining part with a minimum of gold loss. An increase in the deficit might compel the Administration to engage in major retrenchments in its overseas military and foreign aid expenditures for balance-of-payments reasons, or to reverse past policies favoring general lowering of barriers to trade and international capital movements. Such retrenchments or reversals in policy, at a time when de Gaulle and others in Europe are questioning the firmness of U.S.

---

would raise incomes per head by $37 a year, while a 4 percent growth in per capita income in India—more than twice the rate India has experienced—would raise incomes per head by less than $4 a year. In the end, of course, the higher growth rate will close the gap. But it would take seventy-five years, even at this wide differential in rates, before the gap *began* to close, and another forty-five years before it would be eliminated.

[8] I dismiss as unlikely the theoretical possibility that faster growth could reduce imports by generating substitutes for imports faster than rising incomes tend to raise them.

commitment to the defense and welfare of Europe, could weaken greatly the U.S. position of leadership, particularly in dealing with our major allies.

A worsening in the U.S. balance-of-payments deficit caused by policies to stimulate growth might therefore negate some or all of the value to be gained in our international position from more rapid growth. Two questions need to be asked: How much can faster U.S. growth be expected to worsen the balance of payments? What steps can be taken to minimize any adverse impact?

A. *Growth and the Balance of Payments.* The fact that faster growth will stimulate imports from the less-developed countries can be dismissed as a direct source of balance-of-payments embarrassment to the United States. These countries need the additional export earnings to pay for a burgeoning demand for imports, and hence will tend to spend additional earnings promptly. The critical question is whether they are spent in the United States or the other industrial (and re-serve-accumulating) countries. In one paradoxical respect, greater U.S. import demand for raw materials and other primary products may actually help the U.S. balance of payments. Firmer primary product prices will mean that Euro-pean purchasers of primary products—Europe imports nearly four times as much of such products as the United States does —will have to pay higher prices than otherwise for them. This will raise primary producers' export earnings still further, and it will also raise European manufacturing costs more than U.S. costs, thus tending to improve the competitive posi-tion of American products.[9]

---

[9] International cost comparisons are difficult to make. In a survey of American-owned firms operating abroad, however, the National Indus-trial Conference Board found that, on average, materials comprise 46 percent of total unit manufacturing costs in Europe, compared with 32 percent on comparable products in the United States. A given rise in materials costs would thus raise European costs more than U.S. costs. See Theodore Gates and Fabian Linden, *Costs and Competition*, N.I.C.B., 1961, p. 29.

Nonetheless, some of the additional export earnings of the less-developed countries will be spent in reserve-accumulating countries and will tend to worsen the U.S. payments deficit. And, of course, higher U.S. incomes will generally raise U.S. imports directly from other industrial countries. How great these import effects will be and how rapidly U.S. exports will rise depend very much on the character of the growth itself. We can draw a distinction between growth-through-saving and growth-through-innovation. The former relies primarily on saving and accumulation of capital to raise output and labor productivity, while the latter emphasizes the steady improvement in technical and organizational knowledge as the principal source for growth in output. It is often argued that growth-through-saving usually hurts the balance of payments, while growth-through-innovation helps it.[10] Indeed, one view places the pre-eminence of the United States in world markets squarely on its high rate of innovation in new products and new production techniques. It is argued that a weakening of this technological lead bears some responsibility for the transformation of dollar shortage in the early fifties to dollar deficits in the late fifties.

The distinction between growth-through-saving and growth-through-innovation blurs in practice. Technological improvements generally require new investment for their implementation. And in a world in which technical change occurs continuously, new investment usually carries some technical improvements with it.

Despite qualifications, the distinction is relevant for a large country with a weak international payments position, for growth generated through technical change is likely to produce new exportable products, while growth deriving largely from capital accumulation lacks this advantage. This suggests that U.S. growth policy should focus as much as possible on

[10] See, for example, C. P. Kindleberger, "Foreign Trade and Growth: Lessons from British Experience Since 1913," *Lloyds Bank Review*, July 1962.

measures which increase the rate and diffusion of technical change rather than on measures designed merely to raise the rate of saving and investment. Furthermore, rapid technical change carries abroad some of the same psychological value that faster growth itself does—provided the technological improvements are not concentrated in the development of substitutes for imported primary products!

A second distinction should be made in assessing the impact of growth on the balance of payments. Higher productivity can be enjoyed in the form of higher money incomes with constant prices, lower prices with constant money incomes, or greater leisure. Productivity growth taken largely as higher money incomes will tend to hurt the balance of payments more than growth which is taken partly in lower prices. The more growth can be channeled into lower prices, the more exports will be stimulated and import growth retarded. The wage-price guide lines enunciated by the President's Council of Economic Advisers in its Annual Report of 1962 were designed at least to keep money incomes within the bounds permitted by productivity growth, partly because of the balance of payments. Lower wage and profit increases would permit lower prices, helping the balance of payments even more.

Improved economic growth in the United States would have one direct bonus for the U.S. balance of payments: Investment in the other industrial countries, especially the reserve-accumulating countries of continental Europe, would be relatively less attractive to Americans.[11] American direct and portfolio investment outflows to Europe have grown enormously since the mid-fifties, from $130 million in 1955 to $1.0 billion in 1960 and $1.8 billion in 1966. This outflow of investment funds has contributed greatly to the balance-of-payments

---

[11] It is important here, as elsewhere, to distinguish growth in capacity from "growth" resulting from better use of existing capacity. An economic recovery raises profits faster than it raises domestic investment, and may well stimulate rather than retard capital outflow, as firms seek outlets for their additional funds.

deficit. Rapidly growing, profitable markets in Europe (aided by tax advantages in some countries and growing tariff discrimination against American goods in the European Economic Community) made investment there irresistible for many U.S. firms and individuals. Livelier markets at home would reduce the search for exceptional profit opportunities abroad and might even attract foreign investment funds to the United States.

Stronger markets for raw materials would, of course, make U.S. investment in overseas extractive industries much more attractive than it has been in the recent past, and we might see a repetition of the 1956–57 direct investment boom, corresponding to heavy demands for materials in the United States and Europe at the time. But, as mentioned earlier, an increased outflow of funds to the less-developed countries (and to Canada) would be far less damaging to the U.S. balance of payments than corresponding outflows to Europe.

B. *International Coordination of Growth Objectives and Policies.* On balance, then, rapid growth in the United States may hurt the balance of payments much less than it would appear at first sight. But any program to raise the rate of growth might well worsen the balance of payments in the first instance; and with the strong tendency to reap the benefits of growing productivity in the form of higher wages and profits rather than lower prices, too rapid growth by any one country might well land it in payments difficulties—as it did Japan in 1961 and Italy in 1963.

The balance of payments impact of growth can be reduced if several countries attempt to sustain a higher rate of growth together. If one country runs into difficulties because it is growing too rapidly, equilibrium can be restored either by slowing its growth or by raising growth in its principal trading partners. In the absence of coordinated measures to keep up growth in all major countries, world growth might well be slowed by successive balance-of-payments difficulties in the countries which are growing "too rapidly."

Identical growth rates in all countries would be neither necessary nor sufficient to eliminate balance-of-payments difficulties. Quite apart from autonomous changes in tastes or in technology resulting in new demands and new products, payments disequilibrium would arise from three sources:

First, the demand for imports may grow at different rates for different countries even when incomes are growing at the same rate. Typically, the demand for foodstuffs grows more slowly than the growth in incomes, for example, while the demand for certain manufactured products grows more rapidly.

Second, and for the same reason, the foreign demand for each country's exports may grow at different rates. A country which specializes in the production and export of potatoes would very likely find its exports trailing behind the growth in world trade—and behind the growth in its own imports.

Finally, the form in which higher productivity is taken will vary from country to country. Higher productivity leading to higher money income will affect the balance of payments very differently from growth passed on to all consumers, including foreign consumers, in the form of lower product prices. And both will differ in their effects from productivity growth taken in the form of more leisure.

"Coordinated" growth objectives thus do not involve identical growth targets for all cooperating countries, either in total output or in productivity or in per capita income. Identity in any one of these would generally result in differences in the others, in any case. Rather, coordinated growth means that when one country seems to be developing a deficit in its international payments because it is growing rapidly, the first question to be asked is not whether it is growing *too* rapidly, but whether its major trading partners are growing too slowly, and what might be done about it. The importance of the agreement in 1961 among the twenty members of the Organization for Economic Cooperation and Development to grow collectively by 50 percent over the decade of the sixties lies not so much in the particular growth target as in the general acceptance of growth as a desirable objective, a public statement of intention to pursue this common objective collectively, and the provision of a forum where economic problems can be discussed jointly as they develop.

If balance-of-payments problems are to be minimized, policy measures to achieve growth, as well as the growth objective itself, must be coordinated. Countries which take greatly divergent measures to accomplish the same objective may find themselves in substantial balance-of-payments surplus or deficit as a result. For instance, a country which relies primarily on a reduction in long-term interest rates to stimulate investment for growth while its trading partners rely primarily on fiscal incentives would find large sums of financial capital moving abroad in search of higher yields.

By the same token, divergent measures can be taken deliberately to reduce existing imbalances. At the present time, the United States should avoid those growth-inducing measures which might aggravate its still precarious balance-of-payments position. In particular, fiscal incentives should be used in preference to low long-term interest rates to stimulate investment. The investment tax credit and revised depreciation guide lines installed in 1962 were both measures designed specifically to increase the profitability of all new domestic investment. Special fiscal incentives to induce technical innovation in the nonmilitary areas of the economy might be developed more than they have been. In continental Europe, by contrast, a shift in growth policies from heavy reliance on tax privileges and other special incentives to lower long-term interest rates would contribute to international equilibrium.

V . SUMMARY

A more rapid rate of growth in the United States would serve American foreign policy in three ways. First, it would increase the resources that are available in the future to serve our international objectives, and in particular the resources available for national security expenditures and for foreign assistance to the less-developed countries. Economic adjustment to partial or complete disarmament, if that should be the course taken in military expenditures, would be considerably easier in a fully employed, rapidly growing economy than in a slack or a stagnant one.

Second, a higher rate of growth in the United States would raise exports of the less-developed countries, would firm the prices of primary products, and would reduce the pressures for tariff protection against growing imports of manufactures from the developing areas.

Third, high growth would improve the "image" of the United States abroad, thereby aiding those friendly and confounding those hostile to America and to Western values; and at home, the sense of frustration, the search for scapegoats, and the national alternation between retreat to isolationism and forays into aggressive action which could accompany a steady series of reverses in the unsought economic and technological race with the Soviet Union might be avoided.

More rapid growth in the United States need not weaken the precarious U.S. balance-of-payments position. If it did do so, several of the above-mentioned gains from growth might be lost. But growth based as much as possible on innovation, growth that results in some lowering of product prices, growth that is undertaken in collaboration with other like-minded countries—such growth need not be limited by balance-of-payments constraints.

Part VI

Recent U.S. Economic Growth and the Gain in Human Welfare

BY

Robert J. Lampman

In 1947 the Gross National Product of the U.S. was $234 billion; in 1964 it was $600 billion. But over that period the population increased by 46 million, from 144 to 190 million; the consumer price level rose 38 percent; taxes went up from $54 billion to over $150 billion; personal indebtedness increased from $50 billion to over $250 billion; millions of people moved from rural to urban settings and occupations; many married women went to work; the unemployment rate was gradually rising over the period, and in a typical year about 15 percent of the labor force experienced some involuntary unemployment, and dramatic alterations in consumer goods and in style of life occurred.

In the face of these and other changes, is it possible to make a quantitative appraisal of the change in welfare for the representative American? Can we compare the realized change in welfare with a hypothetical gain or loss that might have been associated with some other assumed pattern of change? The answer to both questions is no. No precise measure of absolute or relative welfare or well-being or satisfactions has yet been contrived. The best that can be done is to give rough indicators of costs and benefits experienced by human beings in the process of economic growth. Some of these indicators are to be found in the national income accounts.

I

The GNP is an accounting for one year of the market value of goods and services purchased by consumers for final use, of goods and services purchased by governments for current and future use, and of durable goods purchased by businesses and not charged to current expense. This concept admittedly provides only a crude indication of changes in well-being. It can be refined to bring us closer to an accounting of how the individual is affected. Thus, the GNP can be divided by the total population to show a GNP per person of $3,160 in 1964. While GNP more than doubled in the 1947–64 period, the per capita GNP less than doubled, as shown in Table 1.

TABLE 1

Selected Data on Production, Consumption, and Income, 1947 and 1962

(in 1962 dollars)

Item	1947	1962	% Change 1947–62
(1) Gross National Product (GNP)	234	555	137
(2) GNP per capita	1626	2968	82
(3) adjusted for price change	2341	2968	27
(4) Personal income per consumer unit, before tax	4130	7140	72
(5) after tax	4910	6400	30
(6) Personal consumption per capita	1148	1905	67
(7) adjusted for price change	1515	1905	26
(8) Government purchases per capita of educational, health, medical, and other welfare services	50	157	174
(9) adjusted for price change	66	157	138
(10) All government nondefense purchases per capita	97	352	263
(11) adjusted for price change	127	352	177
(12) Row 7 + Row 11	1642	2257	37

Adjusting for price change in turn further reduces the recorded rise in per capita GNP from nearly 100 percent to 27 percent. It is not a simple matter to adjust GNP for price change. For one thing, the postwar price change is very different by sector of the economy: For consumer purchases it is 24 percent, for investment goods it is 61 percent, and for government purchases it is most severe of all—76 percent. The adjustments for price tells us how much less of an unchanging basket of standard goods one could buy in 1964 than in 1947 if he had a fixed dollar income. It screens out the effect of all price increases, whether arising either out of monetary policy or out of cost-raising business practices (such as greater outlay on advertising) or out of higher taxes on business.

A percentage change in GNP might misrepresent the change in consumer well-being because it includes the production of nonconsumer goods. That is, it includes the value of new factories built during the year, all expenses of the military establishment, and other government purchases, and the value of goods exported. If we confine our attention to private consumption expenditures (which run about 60–67 percent of GNP) we get a less impressive absolute change in production. In 1947, per capita personal consumption was $1,515; in 1962, it was $1,905 (both in 1962 prices). However, the relative increase was 26 percent, about the same as in per capita GNP.

But it is not reasonable to exclude all government purchases from consideration. Many government purchases are clearly and directly instrumental to human well-being. There is a technical point to be cleared up first. In deflating private consumption for price rise, we took out the indirect purchase (through higher prices occasioned by higher taxes) of goods and services used by governments—purchases which can be thought of as collective or social consumption. Hence, it is not double-counting to add such governmental purchases (as distinct from transfers and subsidies) to the deflated personal consumption estimate. It is, however, hard to judge what government purchases to include. Perhaps a maximum total would be all nondefense purchases. A minimum total would be only those for health, education, and welfare. In 1962, the broadest definition shows $352 per person; the narrowest, $157. Social consumption by either concept (we are bypassing the question of whether some of these expenditures should be classified as investment) has been expanding rapidly in the postwar period —more than doubling, even after adjustment for population and price changes. If we count all nondefense government purchases as adding to consumer welfare, we find an increase of 37 percent in what can be called private and collective consumption.

In summary, by various measures it can be shown that per capita consumption expenditures increased between 26 and 37 percent over the period 1947–62—or at an annual rate between 1.5 and 2.5 percent.

It is a good first approximation that change in price-adjusted per capita consumption, including collective consumption, indicates change in welfare. There are, however, numerous objections to this which deserve careful consideration. If accepted, some of these objections would lead to the conclusion that the consumption data overstate, others to the conclusion that they understate, the increase in welfare in postwar years.

First off, there are considerations urged by the experts in national income accounting, who point out that the consumption measure cannot account for the welfare gain arising out of the introduction of new products. Hence, any gain from the introduction of color television or of new "wonder drugs" which is in excess of gain that would have accompanied equal addition to expenditure on the 1947 pattern of consumption is not shown in the consumption figures reported in Table 1. Similarly, there is an understatement to the extent that the quality of given consumer goods and services has been improved. For example, the changing effectiveness of an hour's time in a physician's office is not reflected in the consumption data. Some critics have alleged that the change in products and in quality of products and services is so favorable to consumers as to cancel out the effects of postwar inflation. They contend that the gain in welfare is best indicated by the consumption per capita data unadjusted for price. That would mean not a 26–37 percent gain, but a 67–81 percent gain in the 1947–62 period.

On the other hand, the change in consumption tends to overstate the gain in welfare because it fails to account for the decline in nonmarketed product which has occurred. The national income accounts do not record the net decline in home activities such as gardening, canning, food preparation, sewing, and woodcutting. This decline is associated with the migration from rural to urban areas and the shift from home to paid employment for women. A related point is that the changed style of life, particularly the shift to more densely populated areas, has made certain consumer expenditures (e.g., charges for garbage disposal and for commuting) mandatory rather than optional and hence should not, perhaps, be counted as consumer gain. It is not possible to quantify the importance of this change in the "framework of needs" which has occurred.

I I

Implicit in this discussion is the judgment that some patterns of growth are more productive of human welfare than others. At most, a rise in GNP, even a rise in price-adjusted per capita consumption, points toward the attainment of only one of a constellation of goals. A well-functioning economy allocates and uses its resources efficiently toward the production of things most wanted. It also achieves a fair sharing of output and opportunities to participate. Growth of per capita output may be said to contribute to human welfare only if it means not only more, but more of the goods people want, no less efficient methods of allocation and production, and no less satisfactory sharing of output and of opportunities.

The complexity is suggested by Table 2. Variables related to the several goals are shown down the left-hand side. Whether or not each is changing may be specified in the right-hand column. This table shows the various possible combinations and growth patterns. For example, per capita income and con-

TABLE 2

Schema of Alternative Patterns of Economic Growth

Variables Indicating Change in Human Well-being	Increase or Decrease

Output
Per capita production and income
Per capita consumption
Efficiency
Percent of population in labor force
Percent of labor force employed
Average hours of work
Distribution
Inequality of income distribution
Inequality of wealth distribution
Number of persons in poverty
Composition of output
Shares of public vs. private purchase
Shares of investment vs. consumption
Shares of "investment in human beings" vs.
   "consumption of things"
Other variables
Rate of population growth
Percent of population in urban communities
Numbers of occupational and geographic moves
Percent of labor force self-employed
Degree of governmental planning, direction,
   regulation

sumption could be increasing along with increasing population, a declining employment ratio, a fixed pattern of inequality, and a fixed composition of output. But in every case, if we are to identify the situation as one of economic growth, there must be increase in per capita production and income.

One would be rash to assent to the proposition that each and every growth pattern represented by the table is "good" or desirable. Most of us accept some particular growth pattern. At the same time, most of us would be willing to make some trade-off between a given change in the growth rate of per capita income and any one of the other variables. If a 1 percent increase in per capita income is to be associated with (or followed by) a 2 percent increase in the population, some might say that the price of higher income is too great in terms of congestion or loss of elbow room. Or if high growth requires a radical shift out of balance of the public-private mix, others might say they would prefer a slower growth of living standard in order to reduce the degree of centralization.

This line of thought takes us naturally to a consideration of the costs of growth. It is sometimes implied that growth means more output for less input, and that it is therefore "free" and hence unobjectionable. And this is true to a high degree concerning past growth. The young inherit the accumulated capital and productivity of today's economy "cost-free," but to maintain a constant per capita growth rate we must have more each year per person of some of the inputs of capital, labor effort, enterprise, or technical change. And, as I mentioned earlier, growth means change in the pattern of output. Hence, we must accept changes of many sorts. We must sacrifice some individual security, some of our claims to protection, priority, and precedence. We must be prepared to change occupation, to move from one place to another, to accept loss of status or prestige, if not of income.

Growth means an emphasis upon newness, diversity, and variety—in a word, change. It gives free rein to the process of creative destruction managed by a minority group of aggressive, often youthful, innovators and directed against an entrenched majority. This process sets up internal stresses and dislocations which may be more than a society can survive. One such stress may be on the distribution of income. Solow says "the real hard question about economic growth [is] can industrial countries tease out the investment required for growth by conventional monetary and fiscal policies . . . without twisting the distribution of income in a way that public sentiment finds inadmissible?" But the distribution of income may not reflect all the social stress associated with a sacrifice of familiar patterns, of custom and tradition.

On the larger scene, economic growth has necessitated or has been associated with such imponderables as the growth of large cities, the shift of employment into the large, faceless corporation, the decline of self-employment, and the expansion of the bureaucratic state. Growth has brought with it the assembly line and the computer. It has meant the decline of the extended family, loss of sense of community, the reduction of regional and ethnic diversity.

Some people may prefer less change than a 2 percent rate of growth implies. Growth and change churn up new opportunities for achievement by alert individuals. But we are not unitary in our interests. Not all people thrill to the blend of inputs and outputs associated with growth. The old and the young have different bases for valuing present as contrasted with future consumption. Those who have "arrived" view it one way; those who are seeking a route to economic success see it in a different light. The educated and skilled workers have different reasons for apprehension about technical change than do the unskilled and uneducated. Not all who enjoy the benefits are expected to pay the costs of growth. For some the price of growth is fully compatible with their own life plans and hence is not a price or cost at all. They want to save, to work hard, to attain education, skill, and responsibility. They delight in accommodating change. They have little reverence for the old and traditional ways. The doctrine of growth is an apologia for those whose preferred way of life it befits.

At the same time, however, that growth brings problems for some, it brings a following tide which eases many problems including those it creates. It yields public funds (tax revenues rise as a function of higher national income) to mitigate its own social costs. Economic success has been the anvil against which social protest has pounded out human gains.

The full accounting for the significance of change must balance the dividends of growth against the costs. It must compare the glories of new frontiers with the decline of old patterns. It must compare the problems of a static society with those of a dynamic one. In general, Americans have been disposed to seek the pattern of problems associated with change. We have assumed we can stand progress.

Did the growth in production in the 1947–62 period cost us heavily in terms of sacrifice of other goals? It does not seem to me that it did. On the contrary, it was associated with remarkable gains on numerous fronts.

The age-adjusted death rate fell from 10.1 to 9.5 per 1,000 between 1947 and 1962. The infant mortality rate dropped from 32.2 to 25.3 in the same period. The average size of family has stayed well above prewar levels, but now the size of family is more nearly associated with size of income. The percent of married couples with their own household (that is, not living with relatives) went up from 91.4 to 97.9. Home-ownership rose from 53 percent of all occupied dwelling units to 61 percent; ownership of automobiles from 54 to over 75 percent of families. Growth has meant a narrowing of differences in life styles, a democratization of consumption patterns. The percent of income spent on food by the lowest fifth of income receivers declined from 35 to 29 percent. And 90 percent of American homes have electric washing machines, refrigerators, and television sets; 115 million persons are life insurance policy-holders, over 12 million persons own shares in public corporations. Recent years have continued a trend toward a more equalitarian distribution of leisure with shorter hours of work, more paid vacations, and earlier retirement for many workers. The percent of youngsters 14–17 years of age who were in school changed from 82 in 1947 to 92 in 1962.

The 37 percent increase in consumption occurred without a reduction in personal saving. Indeed, personal saving, which was abnormally high in World War II, and which fell to a low of about 4 percent in the early postwar years, had stabilized by the late fifties at about 7 percent of disposable personal income. This improved savings ratio was associated with a rapidly accumulating total of personally owned wealth, which in 1962 amounted to about $2 trillion. This was more than $10,000 of assets per capita. It is true that personal debt has increased rapidly in recent years. Persons owed debts (including short-term and mortgage debt) in the amount of $246 billion, or $1,300 per capita. Hence, net worth per capita was about $8,700.

The rise in consumption and saving was coupled with a gain in still another component of welfare—income security. The risk of loss of income due to the hazards of old age, unemployment, disability, and premature death of family breadwinner was progressively better insured. Public income maintenance benefits under social insurance and public assistance programs (particularly those aimed at the old-age hazard) were increased dramatically during the 1950's. These benefits rose from $9 billion in 1950 to $32 billion in 1962. They amounted to 3 percent of GNP in 1950 and over 5 percent in 1962.

It is interesting to note that these advances came about with only minor change in another welfare indicator—the size distributions of income and wealth. Rising affluence probably made the persisting pattern of inequality less sensitive as a social issue. The top 5 percent of income receivers got about 18 percent of "after tax family personal income" in each of the years under consideration; the lowest 20 percent got around 5 percent. There is considerable evidence that the top group had experienced a fall in share of income and wealth in years before 1949. But it appears that this trend toward less inequality stopped and perhaps reversed by 1949. In my own study, I found that the top 2 percent of wealth-holders held 29 percent of all wealth in 1949; this had risen to 30 percent by 1956. This trend was confirmed by the University of Michigan Survey of Consumer Finances which found that the top decile of wealth-holders had 58 percent of net worth in 1953, 61 percent in 1962. The lowest fifth of income receivers had 11 percent of net worth in 1953, 7 percent in 1962.

Although there was some disquieting news from the inequality front, the growth in per capita income, consumption, and wealth was associated with a remarkable drop in the numbers of persons in low-income or poverty status. Using a $3,000 income (1962 prices) for families as the dividing mark for poverty, the number of families in poverty fell from 12

million in 1947 to 9.3 million in 1962 and to 9.1 million in
1963. This was a drop from 32 to 19 percent of all families.

III

In the preceding section I noted that growth in per capita consumption is always accompanied by costs and may require the
foregoing of certain goals. However, I asserted that the costs
experienced in the period under study were more than offset
by the gains. In recent years, growth of consumption has been
accompanied by such indications of gain in well-being as more
leisure, more wealth, more income security, and a lower incidence of poverty. Hence, we tentatively conclude that the
increase in per capita consumption is a fair, though rough and
incomplete, indicator of gain in human well-being in postwar
America.

However, some economists would shy away from drawing
this conclusion. They would say that as "scientists" we should
avoid making value judgments of this sort. They would point
out that in a free society the ultimate value of the observed
growth in consumption is hidden in the subjective calculus of
the free participants who individually evaluate economic results and the cost of achieving them. They fear that it is only
a short jump from the judgment that more consumption means
more welfare, to advocacy of a plan to achieve more consumption.

To see the full force of this line of thought, envision, if you
will, the economy as a huge system for translating inputs of
land, labor, and capital (valued by free suppliers) into outputs of goods and services (valued by free consumers). The
system is efficient to the degree that it approaches maximum
value of output from a given value of input. The sovereign
consumer and the supplier of inputs, through an interrelated
network of markets, simultaneously decide how to produce
and distribute how much of what kind of output. Individuals

change the capacity to produce by decisions to save, to invest in plant and equipment or in education, to do research and inventive work, and the like. Growth in actual output follows increases in capacity to produce only if consumers want more of one product and no less of another. The growth rate that arises out of this process of individual decision-making is, by the definition some would use, the "right" rate, and the gain in welfare is the "right" gain. From this point of view there cannot be a superior collective wisdom on the appropriate rate of growth any more than on the choice between red and blue automobiles. In the extreme formulation of this picture, a social judgment about rate of growth is considered to be redolent of a centrally managed society.

A humanitarian and a democrat must accept a considerable part of that formulation of the economic process. It is a valuable caution against easy acceptance of the idea that a higher rate of growth is always indicative of a greater gain in human welfare than is a lower rate. There are, of course, objections to this line of thinking which elevates freedom for the individual to an exclusive principle. It leaves no room for collective purposes, such as national defense, which can only be financed by public provision. It overlooks the familiar fact of external effects of individual decisions. Because of these effects, I am interested not only in my own but also in my neighbor's consumption and capacity to produce. And because I am interested in the future well-being of my children, I am interested in the future well-being of his. To the extent that our decisions about economic growth constitute a treaty across the generations, some degree of collective judgment may be called for. Further, the fact is that public policy does presently bear upon changes in the nation's capacity to produce. In virtually every market, government participates or intervenes, and such intervention does have an effect on growth. Hence, we do need a community judgment on the relative value of growth.

Economic growth, under our system, is limited to what can be validated by free consumer choice and democratic assent to collective purchase. Changes in the capacity to produce are primarily the result of choices which, while significantly conditioned by public policy, are choices made by free individuals. We conclude that, so long as this is the case, there is merit to the use of economic growth as one indicator, along with others, of gain in human well-being.

When all is said and done, the American system turns back to free choice of the individual consumer, voter, and producer for legitimation. And economic growth will draw its vitality from those sources. It is precisely because of the role played by the consumer that some critics would undercut the use of the growth rate as an indicator of gain in well-being. They would say that more consumption does not lead to more welfare because consumers' wants are not genuine, spontaneous, and independent, but are contrived and synthesized by producers and sellers of goods. The sovereign consumer is, it is alleged, really a dancing puppet responding to strings manipulated by monopolistic manufacturers and their Madison Avenue lackeys. The lackeys, it is claimed, mislead and misinform the consumer concerning the goods they sell, and cause wants to flower in the consumer desert where none had bloomed before by urging buyers to keep up with, or get ahead of, the Joneses. Consumers are mass-persuaded into a self-defeating pattern of style-conscious, invidious, conspicuous consumption financed by mass indebtedness. The sacred consumer-wants, for which the vast machinery of the economy is marshaled, are thus represented as unworthy. The "sovereign" is seen as bewitched by his "subjects." Production is conducted for the benefit of producers. Consumption becomes not the purpose for, but the fuel of the productive process, and bears little relationship to human welfare.

One has to evaluate this as meaningful characterization or caricature by his own lights. My own judgment is that, while there is an uncomfortably high degree of truth in it, it remains essentially a caricature. It is true that consumption is a relatively backward art, and that the range of goods and services offered to the consumer makes informed choice expensive in terms of time and effort. However, it is my belief that consumers do progressively better over time in allocating their expenditures, and that increased consumption does represent increased satisfaction or welfare.

But there is a more cogent point, having to do with the diminishing utilities of extra income, which argues that recent and future growth is far less important than earlier growth from much lower levels of income, and hence that the 2 percent per year rate of growth in per capita consumption tends relatively to overstate the gain in welfare. There can be little doubt of the human values of growth where the common pattern is at or near subsistence and where the largest part of increased production is devoted to a gain in elementary physical well-being—reduction of morbidity and mortality. In that case growth is life-giving and life-saving, restorative if not redemptive, permissive if not creative. To question growth there is to question the value of life itself.

But by what license do we proclaim the value of additions to income and wealth in an already rich nation? Is it possible that the 1947–62 increase in per capita consumption meant only a 10 or 15 percent increase in total welfare? Is it possible that the prior increase of income may have carried the representative family to the point where further pursuit of such income yields far less of basic value than some alternative use of time and energy? Presumably the most urgent needs have long since been met. We know that a person misses a great deal if all he does is work and save and invest and accumulate. Could not also a nation misallocate its energy in an unbalanced or obsessive attention to production as opposed to consumption, leisure, and other aspects of a good life?

But not all of us are rich. Talk of the representative American disregards those who have far less of the material things of life than the average man. Few would argue that at least the poor among us have high value uses for extra income. As noted above, the growth in per capita income in the postwar period has resulted in a substantial reduction of the number and percent of persons in poverty. The decline from 12 million to 9.3 million families with less than $3,000 incomes of 1962 purchasing power is a signal accomplishment of our economy. To continue this reduction is a prime reason for encouraging further economic growth. If we can continue the 1947–62 rate of growth, the number of poor families should decline to 7 million, or 12 percent of all families by 1975.

While growth in per capita income and production is not the only factor in the reduction of poverty, it is clear that the rate of reduction responds to changes in the rate of growth. Between 1947 and 1957, when per capita income grew at a rate of 3 percent per year, the percent of families in poverty fell from 32 to 23. Between 1957 and 1962, when income grew at a rate of only 2 percent, the percent in poverty fell only from 23 to 20 percent. Hence, it would appear that a substantial number of families, perhaps 2 percent of the total, were held back to poverty levels of living by the failure of the economy to grow at a higher rate in the more recent years.

At present over half of the 9.3 million poor families are in a position to benefit directly from a higher rate of economic growth. They have one or more members of their family employed or otherwise in the labor force. More employment or opportunity to work at more productive jobs will provide many of them with escapes from poverty. A growing economy continually provides incentive for employers to adapt and train workers for higher-paying jobs. Jobs are redefined, assignments are redistributed in such a way as to break down traditional barriers against nonwhites and other disadvantaged groups.

It is true that there are some groups in poverty, most notably the aged and broken families, who are relatively immune to economic growth because they are not part of the labor force. For these groups, growth will make only indirect contributions. It will produce the public revenues which are necessary for higher social insurance and public assistance benefits whereby poverty can be relieved. It can offer the means for ever-larger parts of the population to insure themselves against those retreats into poverty which follow the contingencies of disability, premature death of the family breadwinner, and old age. Over the longer run, growth can provide the revenues for the improved schooling, and health, environment, and training opportunities by which life chances for those born poor can be bettered. It is an important fact that fully one-third of the present poor are children.

But the poor are not alone in their interest in higher incomes. There is even some reason to doubt that the typical American family has reached the point of sharply diminishing utility of extra income. Currently the median family income is about $6,000. At present rates of change it will be about $9,000 in 1984. The case for sustained growth is that it is important that it be $9,000 instead of $8,000. Doubtless few would argue that the extra $1,000 is as important as was the $1,000 which raised the medium to $6,000. The ninth thousand dollars will go to satisfying less critical needs, but those needs are still worth satisfying and should not be disregarded. We would observe with McCracken that, while this is an era when it has been fashionable to speak in a deprecatory way about the alleged unseemly, tail-fin affluence of the economy's "private sector," ". . . it should strain no one's imagination to believe that [the] average American family could produce quite a long list of very commendable items that it would like to buy if there were a little more of this thing darkly referred to as private affluence."

The goods and services to which people devote an increasing share of income as they get richer include not only second automobiles but better health care, education, recreation, travel, and artistic expression. They also include public expenditures for urban redevelopment, better schools and hospitals, safer streets and roads, better water supply, and freedom from air pollution.

Growth of productive capacity is of value precisely because

it gives us more options. Growth of income, by reducing the death rate, frees resources from replacing the population for the improvement of it. Thus freedom, which consists of the possession of reasonable alternatives, is enlarged. A higher standard of living is ultimately justified by the opportunity it gives to individuals to so conduct their lives in freedom and responsibility as to attain what John Stuart Mill referred to as development of all their faculties.

I V

This paper opened with the suggested question, does recent U.S. economic growth indicate gain in human welfare? I have answered by asserting that the change in price-adjusted per capita private and collective consumption is a rough first approximation to such an indicator. It shows a 37 percent gain between 1947 and 1962, or about 2 percent per year. There has been a psychological cost to the rapid social change associated with growth. It is a cost which is uneven in impact. However, income security has been improved, and while inequality of wealth and income has not decreased, the number of persons in poverty has been significantly reduced.

Growth is given its chief claim to legitimacy as an indicator of well-being by the free choices of consumers, workers, and citizens. That these choices are subject to improvement through continued experiment and learning does not invalidate the growth measure.

While there is plausibility to the idea that the growth of recent years overstates (relative to similar growth in earlier periods) the gain in welfare because of a possible diminishing utility of the successive additions to consumption, it is not fully persuasive because of the progress which the added product has enabled against poverty and by the shift to a number of goods and services, including education, which are believed to have high social value. By opening new choices, growth has improved the chances of many persons for what an old Greek definition says is happiness, "The exercise of vital powers along lines of excellence in a life affording them scope."

Economic growth is not the same thing as—and is not always associated with—net gain in human welfare. However, it seems clear that, all things considered, the pattern of growth in the United States in the postwar years yielded benefits to individuals far in excess of the costs it required of them. To that extent our material progress has had humane content.

Part VII

Investments in Human Capital and Economic Growth

BY

William G. Bowen

Formal education in schools, informal education in the home, on-the-job training, health research and health services—all of these constitute "investments in human capital" in that they increase the economic capabilities of people over a long period of time. This is not to say that these "human investments" are made solely for materialistic reasons; education and health are generally thought to be important elements of "the good life" and would undoubtedly be accorded a very high priority by many of us even if no economic payoff were involved. But some of the most eloquent statements on behalf of the noneconomic contributions of education and health go so far as to deny that economic effects are of any relevance at all; and surely this kind of emphasis is just as one-sided as interpretations which stress only effects on physical output.

Investments in human capital are like investments in physical capital in important respects. Both accrue as a result of the application of economic resources (buildings, materials, skilled labor) which could have been used to produce other goods and services for immediate enjoyment; both yield streams of benefits over long periods of time; and yet both do have a finite life-span—machines wear out and men die.

These similarities are worth noting because concepts such as rates of return, developed in the main to explain the economics of investments in physical capital, can also be helpful in assessing the economic effects of investments in human capital.

The most significant difference between human investments and physical investments is that while a piece of machinery exists only to supply economic services and does not suffer pain or pleasure in the process, investments in education and health are inseparable from the human beings in which they are embodied. Engineers are hired by firms, not purchased outright; they may quit if they feel they are being mistreated, if they think they would be better off working elsewhere, or for no apparent reason at all. And, as we shall see later in this paper, the fact that human capital cannot be bought and sold (which is another way of saying that slavery is illegal) has important implications for the economics of investments in human capital.

The importance of human capital to the economy of a country has been recognized for a long time. Both Adam Smith and Alfred Marshall had a good deal to say about investments of the human variety. However, it is also true that only in the last decade or so has this subject received heavy emphasis.[1]

[1] Credit for directing recent attention to the role of human investments in the growth process is shared by J. W. Kendrick, *et al.* of the National Bureau of Economic Research, Edward Denison of the Brookings Institution, T. W. Schultz of the University of Chicago, and Gary Becker of Columbia University. Kendrick's empirical work showed that only a surprisingly small fraction of the total increase in this country's GNP could be attributed to increases in the quantities of labor and physical capital, the remainder presumably being due mainly to new knowledge and to the increased health, vitality, and ability of the population. (See his *Productivity Trends in the United States,* Princeton University Press for the N.B.E.R., 1961.) In Denison's widely acclaimed study, *The Sources of Economic Growth in the United States* (CED, January 1962), investments in human capital show up in two ways: (a) as direct returns to formal education; and (b) as part of Denison's residual, which he regards as the result of "advances in knowledge." Schultz has focused most directly on the costs and benefits associated with formal education, and has not only done significant work of his own but has also stimulated others to work in this area. (See, for example, his presidential address delivered to the American Economic Association, "Investment in Human Capital," *American Economic Review,* March 1961, pp. 1–17.) Becker has done important theoretical and empirical work on the returns to investments in human capital, and he is about to publish a book on this subject.

In this brief essay, I shall first discuss the overall magnitude of our investments in human capital, then examine the evidence as to the relation between past investments in human capital and economic growth, and end with a discussion of policy issues.

I. COST ESTIMATES

How much has this country been spending on education and health? Anyone who claims to have a precise, unambiguous answer, in which he has complete confidence, is surely a charlatan. If estimating the cost of most any economic activity can be described as difficult, estimating the cost of investments in human capital can certainly be described as *very* difficult.

The extra degree of difficulty here is due to the existence (and great quantitative importance) of foregone output. The presumption is that a student who goes on to college could have gone straight to work instead, and therefore the costs to society of providing a college education consist not only of direct costs (salaries of teachers and the like) but also of indirect costs—the additional output that could have been produced had time not been invested in studying. Similarly, a person who goes to a doctor for treatment incurs not only the direct cost represented by the doctor's bill, but also the indirect cost of having spent time in the doctor's office which could have been devoted to other pursuits.

Nor is the direct-cost aspect of investments in human capital entirely straightforward, but here at least there are regularly published data which serve as a starting point. Table 1 contains some estimates of aggregate direct expenditures, private and public, for education and health, for selected years from 1929–30 through 1964–65.[2] As this table indicates, total direct

[2] I am indebted to Mrs. Virginia Gebhardt and Mrs. Clelia Casey for assistance in compiling these data as well as other figures presented later in this chapter.

TABLE 1

Direct Expenditures (Public and Private) on Health and Formal Education
Selected Fiscal Years 1929–30—1964–65[a]

(in Millions of Current Dollars)

	1929–30[b]	1939–40	1949–50	1959–60	1961–62	1962–63	1963–64	1964–65[c]
Health Expenditures[d]	3,613	3,864	12,120	26,559	30,570	32,940	35,462	38,308
Formal Education Expenditures:[e]								
Elementary and Secondary	2,601	2,594	6,672	18,106	20,891	22,960[c]	24,900[c]	26,900[c]
Higher	503	605	2,123	5,529	7,090	7,480[c]	9,223[c]	10,100[c]
Total	3,104	3,199	8,795	23,635	27,981	30,440	34,123	37,000
Total Health and Education	6,717	7,063	20,915	50,194	58,551	63,380	69,585	75,308
Health as % of GNP[f]	3.7	4.1	4.5	5.4	5.7	6.0	5.8	5.6
Education as % of GNP	3.2	3.4	3.2	4.8	5.2	5.6	5.6	5.4
Total as % of GNP[g]	6.9	7.4	7.7	10.2	10.8	11.6	11.4	11.1
Gross Private Domestic Investment (GPDI)[f]	13,300	11,300	41,500	72,600	77,400	85,000	89,900	99,800
Health and Education as % of GPDI	50.5	62.5	50.4	69.1	75.6	74.6	77.4	75.5

[a] Source: Calculated from U.S. Department of Health, Education and Welfare, Trends, 1963 ed., pp. 60, 63; 1965 ed., pp. 25, 61, 64; and Economic Report of the President, 1967 ed. Table B-1, p. 213.

[b] For 1929–30 the health figures are for fiscal year 1929 and education figures for academic year 1929–30.

[c] Preliminary estimates.

[d] Health figures exclude school health expenses; these are included in the education figures. There may be some research expenditures included in the health figures which are also included in the education data.

[e] Education expenditures exclude auxiliary expenses (i.e., student aid and dormitory facilities, etc.). Auxiliary expenses for 1964–65 are estimated at $2 billion.

[f] GNP and GPDI figures are the average for the two calendar years.

[g] May not total, due to rounding.

expenditures on health and education increased from $6.7 billion in 1929–30 to $75 billion in 1964–65. Inflation and the general growth of the economy are of course reflected in these figures, and to obtain a clearer picture of the growth of expenditures in these areas relative to the economy as a whole, it is more instructive to express direct health and education expenditures as a percentage of the GNP. This has been done in the middle panel of Table 1, and we see that these expenditures amounted to about 7 percent of the GNP in 1929–30, to about 10 percent in 1959–60, and to around 11 percent in recent years.

Lest anyone think that the education figures have been inflated by such things as big-time football and palatial housing for undergraduates, I hasten to point out that "auxiliary expenses" of educational institutions have been excluded from these figures. Furthermore, no attempt has been made to add any imputed value for property tax or sales tax exemptions.

To the direct costs of education must be added an estimate of the value of the additional output that could have been produced had students worked rather than gone to school. Two estimates are available for the year 1955–56. Schultz estimates output foregone by high school and college students at about $12 billion while Blitz arrives at an $18-billion estimate.[3]

Both Schultz and Blitz approach this estimation problem by equating the value of the output that students might have produced with the earnings that the students would have received had they been employed rather than in school. The major explanation for the substantial difference in their estimates is that Schultz assumes that young people in high school and college would have had the same earnings as

[3] T. W. Schultz, "Capital Formation by Education," *Journal of Political Economy*, December 1960, pp. 571–83; and Rudolph C. Blitz, "The Nation's Educational Outlay," in U.S. Department of Health, Education, and Welfare, *Economics of Higher Education*, 1962, pp. 147–69 and 390–403. See also T. W. Schultz, *The Economic Value of Education*, Columbia University Press, 1963, Chap. 2, especially pp. 35–36.

young people of the same age not in high school or college, while Blitz assumes that the students, because of their greater native ability, would have earned more had they been in the labor force than those young people of the same age who did not go on with their schooling.

Five case studies examined by Blitz do support his contention that earnings differences are substantial between students of comparable age who attend high school or college and those who do not; hence, as Schultz himself notes in his summary of the literature on this question, "estimates of earnings foregone based on the earnings of those youths who are not in school to this extent tend to understate the earnings foregone for those attending school." [4] However, Schultz also notes that both his estimate and Blitz' estimate ignore the earnings of students while they are in school. And a recent study by the Bureau of Labor Statistics indicates that such earnings are substantial. This consideration suggests that the Schultz estimate is a bit too low and that the Blitz estimate is a bit too high. Whatever the "best" estimate may be (and I have not tried to come up with an exact figure of my own), the important point for our purposes is that earnings foregone are a very substantial component of the total costs of high school and college education. Indeed, earnings foregone are well over half of the total costs of high school and college education, and probably nearer three-quarters, which in turn means that schools which charge no tuition whatsoever are still far from "free."

All of the above figures are annual flows—that is, they are gross expenditures made in a given year. Since both human and nonhuman capital assets are long-lived, for many purposes it is more useful to know the total stock in existence at a particular point in time than the increment to the stock that occurred during the given year. Schultz has estimated the total value of the stock of education in this country for various

[4] Schultz, *The Economic Value of Education*, pp. 31–32.

years, and has compared the value of this stock with the value of the stock of reproducible nonhuman wealth. He estimates that in 1900 the value of the educational stock of labor fourteen years old and older was about 22 percent of the value of the stock of reproducible nonhuman wealth. Over time, as the figures in the bottom panel of Table 1 show, annual investments in human capital have increased much more rapidly than annual investments in nonhuman capital. And Schultz estimates that by 1957 the value of the educational stock had risen to 42 percent of the value of the stock of physical capital.[5]

II. EVIDENCE AS TO THE RELATION BETWEEN HUMAN CAPITAL AND ECONOMIC GROWTH[6]

The very fact that we have made these substantial investments in human capital indicates that our society has put a high value

[5] Schultz, "Education and Economic Growth" in *Social Forces Influencing American Education*, 60th Yearbook of the National Society for the Study of Education, Pt. 2, p. 73.

[6] This section (and the first part of the next section) are based largely on the first essay in my *Economic Aspects of Education; Three Essays* (Industrial Relations Section, Princeton University Press, 1964). The discussion in the original essay is more detailed and more technical than the discussion presented here.

It should also be noted that the bulk of the discussion below pertains to formal education rather than to health or on-the-job training. While more research has been done in the area of formal education than elsewhere, many of the same principles apply to all types of human investment. (See Gary S. Becker's *Human Capital: A Theoretical and Empirical Analysis, with Special Reference to Education*, N.B.E.R., 1964. The reader interested in the health literature should consult Herbert Klarman, *The Economics of Health*, Columbia University Press, 1965, and also Selma Muskin's "Health as an Investment," *Journal of Political Economy*, October 1962 Supplement, pp. 129–57 and the references cited therein. On-the-job training, migration, and information are also discussed in this same issue by, respectively, Jacob Mincer, Larry Sjaastad, and George Stigler.)

on the overall contribution of education and health. Furthermore, thinking for the moment solely in terms of economic contributions, it is easy to argue *a priori* that expenditures on education and health ought to be expected to raise the quality of people's potential economic performance, and therefore, assuming no adverse effects on their inclination to work, to raise the country's total output. For purposes of policy formation, however, broad statements of this kind are by no means sufficient. *How much* of an economic contribution has been made by investments in human capital? Have we underinvested or overinvested in human capital relative to physical capital? These are the empirical questions which we must answer, as best we can, if discussion of the role of investments in human capital in the growth process is to move beyond the stage of speculation.

Simple Correlations. As a rule, a country with a relatively high output per capita educates a relatively high proportion of its population. Harbison and Myers, in a cross-sectional study of seventy-five countries at different stages of economic development, found a positive correlation of .88 between GNP per capita and a composite index made up of secondary and college-level enrollment ratios.[7]

Correlations of this type cannot, of course, in and of themselves, suffice as evidence of the contribution of education to economic growth because they do not tell us what is cause and what is effect. The positive correlation can be used as evidence in support of the proposition that spending money on education is an important way of raising a country's GNP, or the same correlation can be used in support of the proposition that education is an important consumer good on which countries elect to spend more as their GNP goes up. The

[7] Frederick Harbison and Charles A. Myers, *Education, Manpower and Economic Growth*, McGraw-Hill, 1964, p. 40. As Harbison and Myers emphasize, it would have been better to relate GNP per capita to the *stock* of education, but the required data were simply unavailable. In addition to the Harbison-Myers study, there have been several other intercountry studies of the same type. References are given in footnotes on pp. 23–24 of the Harbison-Myers book.

difficulty is that these propositions are almost certainly both true to some extent—and, in the absence of other information, there is no way of disentangling the cause and effect relationships.

Evidence from Residuals. Indirect evidence as to the economic contribution of investments in human capital has been provided by another type of research, already mentioned briefly in the introduction to this essay. This can be called the "residual approach," and it consists of taking the total increase in economic output of a country over a given period of time, allocating as much of the total increase as possible to measurable inputs (capital and the quantity of labor being the two measurable inputs usually chosen), and then saying that the residual is attributable to the unspecified inputs. Education, on-the-job training, health expenditures, and investments in human capital in general are presumably the most important of the unspecified inputs.

Kendrick, in his N.B.E.R. study, found that for the U.S. economy, over the period between 1889 and 1957, his combined input index increased at an average rate of 1.9 percent per annum and his output index increased about 3.5 percent per annum, leaving a residual increase of about 1.6 percent per annum. Thus, 46 percent of the increase in total output over this period is ascribed to the residual.[8]

Aside from some difficult conceptual issues of a rather tech-

[8] John W. Kendrick, *Productivity Trends in the United States,* N.B.E.R., 1961. The figures are from his Table 6, p. 79. A slightly different version of the residual approach has been adopted by Solow and others, who have made explicit assumptions about the nature of the underlying production function. Dealing with a linear, homogeneous production function, assuming that technical change is "neutral," and working with output per man-hour rather than total output, the residual has been found to equal roughly 90 percent of the increase in output per man-hour in the U.S. economy between 1915 and 1955. (The 90 percent figure is from a paper by B. F. Massell, "Capital Formation and Technological Change in U.S. Manufacturing," *Review of Economics and Statistics,* May 1960, pp. 182–88. Massell adopts the theoretical approach originally used by Solow in his "Technical Change and the Aggregate Production Function," *Review of Economics and Statistics,* August 1957, pp. 312–20.

nical kind (especially the questions of the proper way of measuring capital inputs and of taking account of the presumed complementarity between human capital and physical capital), the main difficulty with this approach is the "residual" nature of the residual. As usually measured, the residual no doubt embodies the results of some secular improvements in the quality of capital assets; it also encompasses changes in output attributable to economies of scale, to improvements in the health of the labor force, to informal as well as formal education, to changes in the product mix, to reorganizations of the economic order, and to who knows what else. Moses Abramovitz has called it a "measure of our ignorance." [9]

The heterogeneity of the elements that go to make up the residual means, of course, that a large residual cannot safely be interpreted as a mandate for more spending on any particular project, whether it be a massive research and development effort or better school lunches. At the same time, the size of the residual certainly does serve as a mandate to explore in detail the economic effects of activities too often neglected by scholars.

Earnings Differentials and Rates of Return. The most direct way in which investments in human capital affect output is by increasing the lifetime productivities of the particular individuals who obtain education and health care; and, in a market economy, increased productivity will be reflected (to some extent, at least) in increased lifetime earnings. This is the rationale for using lifetime earnings differentials between, for instance, college graduates and high school graduates as evidence of the economic contribution of college education.

Investments in human capital can affect lifetime earnings by increasing lifetime labor force participation, by reducing the average amount of unemployment, and by increasing the rate of pay per week worked. Tables 2, 3, and 4 show the simple associations between one type of investment in human capital

[9] *Resources and Output Trends in the U.S. Since 1870,* Occasional Paper 52, N.B.E.R., 1956, p. 11.

TABLE 2

*Labor Force Participation Rates
by Age, Sex and Education*

(March 1965)[a]

Age and Sex	<5	5–7	8	1–3 high school	4 high school	1–3 college	4 college	5+ college
				Years of School Completed				
Males								
25–34	85.3	94.6	97.8	98.3	98.5	96.0	98.2	92.7
35–44	85.1	92.8	95.6	97.2	98.7	98.4	99.5	98.9
45–54	86.0	93.4	94.8	94.9	97.2	98.0	98.2	99.4
55–64	74.1	77.9	85.5	85.3	90.0	90.6	93.9	93.9
65+	17.7	22.9	27.1	35.5	35.1	44.1	41.1	57.5
Females								
25–34	26.6	30.8	35.6	37.6	38.2	38.9	50.2	63.2
35–44	32.3	43.4	47.1	45.8	46.2	39.2	49.9	73.7
45–54	38.7	42.0	47.4	48.1	52.7	51.4	59.4	84.3
55–64	26.0	31.4	37.1	39.6	46.0	46.3	63.1	78.1
65+	7.5	8.1	7.9	11.8	13.8	14.7	20.6	38.7

[a] Source: *Educational Attainment of Workers, March 1965*, Special Labor Force Report No. 65, U.S.D.L., B.L.S., Table E, p. A-10.

—formal education—and labor force participation, unemployment, and mean annual earnings. Even the most cursory examination of these profiles reveals substantial variations according to years of school completed.

To obtain a picture of the *net* economic gains to an individual associated with additional education, it is also necessary to take account of both the direct costs to society of providing education and the opportunity costs entailed in spending time in school rather than in the labor force. It is then possible to calculate the internal rate of return applicable to various increments of education.[10]

[10] This is not the place to discuss in any detail the various technical problems involved in adjusting data and making calculations. Gary Becker's N.B.E.R. study contains a full discussion of these matters. However, there are two points which deserve to be mentioned here. First, cross-sectional estimates of income differentials are likely to

TABLE 3

*Unemployment Rates
by Age, Sex, and Education*

(March 1965)[a]

Age and Sex				Years of School Completed			
	<5	5–7	8	1–3 high school	4 high school	1–3 college	4 college
Males							
25–34	5.5	8.5	6.9	6.3	2.8	2.2	1.2
35–44	5.7	8.1	4.2	5.1	2.3	2.6	1.2
45–54	6.8	6.0	4.5	4.4	2.2	1.7	.4
55–64	6.2	4.8	5.2	4.3	3.0	1.5	1.6
65+	10.8	3.3	3.6	6.0	2.9	5.5	2.4
Females							
25–34	b	7.4	11.1	8.2	5.9	7.0	2.3
35–44	9.9	10.3	5.8	5.3	3.6	2.7	1.5
45–54	12.4	6.0	3.0	5.3	3.1	.2	.8
55–64	4.7	5.1	2.8	5.0	2.1	.6	b
65+	8.5	2.7	2.5	3.8	4.5	b	b

[a] Source: *Educational Attainment of Workers, March 1965*, Special Labor Force Report No. 65, U.S.D.L., B.L.S.. Table K, p. A-14.
[b] Percent not shown where base is less than 100,000.

TABLE 4

*Mean Earnings in 1959 of Males 25–64 in the
Experienced Civilian Labor Force by Age and Education*[a]

(in dollars)

Age			Years of School Completed			
	0–7	8	1–3 high school	4 high school	1–3 college	4+ college
25–34	3,225	4,197	4,783	5,361	5,849	7,053
35–44	3,658	4,730	5,500	6,398	7,846	10,863
45–54	3,759	4,904	5,719	6,691	8,604	13,313
55–64	3,810	4,840	5,762	6,824	8,610	13,089
All ages	3,659	4,725	5,379	6,132	7,401	10,078

[a] Source: U.S. Census, 1960, *Occupation by Earnings and Education*, Final Report PC(2)-7B, Table 1, p. 2.

A number of estimates of the internal rate of return on college education have been made, and while the exact results have varied somewhat depending on the methodology employed, we will not be far off if we take 10 to 12 percent as the usual range.[11]

How seriously one takes these results as evidence of the past contribution of college education to economic progress depends on how one answers the following questions: (1) How much of the apparent returns to education ought really to be attributed to the greater native ability, motivation, etc., of college graduates vis-à-vis high school graduates? (2) To what extent (if at all) are the higher salaries paid college graduates undeserved in terms of actual productivity? (3) Does education increase the output of the country as a whole in indirect ways which do not show up in the earnings differentials enjoyed by college graduates—in the language of the economist, does education generate substantial external benefits? No one claims that any of these three questions have been answered at all conclusively, and it is largely for this reason that intuition continues to play a significant role in assessments of the overall contribution of education to economic growth.

---

understate true, cohort differentials because of the general secular increase in real income—it is absolute differentials, not percentage differentials, that are relevant for calculating returns, and absolute differentials will of course increase over time if average income goes up and percentage differentials are unchanged. Second, the relation between education and labor force participation cannot be ignored—which is what happens when earnings comparisons are restricted to persons who were in the labor force. A related point, already noted earlier, is that it is a mistake to think of being enrolled in school and being in the labor force as mutually exclusive categories—a growing proportion of students earn some income while in school and such earnings of course reduce the opportunity costs of schooling.

[11] See W. Lee Hansen, *Journal of Political Economy*, April 1963, pp. 128–40, and references cited therein. The most thorough analysis of this type is Becker's *Human Capital*. See also the excellent Ph.D. dissertation by Giora Hanech, "Personal Earnings and Investment in Schooling," University of Chicago, 1965. (A summary of Hanech's thesis has been published in *Journal of Human Resources*, Summer 1967.)

There have been a number of "case-study" type investigations of the extent of the interrelation between "ability," education, and earnings; and Becker, on the basis of a review of the relevant literature, concludes that differences in ability per se do *not* account for a large part of the observed earnings differentials between college graduates and high school graduates. Becker estimates that taking account of the ability differentials reduces the true rate of return on college education by only about two percentage points, and that the rate of return earned by urban white males as of 1950 was above 10 percent even after making this adjustment.[12] However, it would be wrong to imply that anyone puts great weight on these precise values, given the problems of measuring "economic ability" and the lack of comprehensive studies. Furthermore, the range of probable error is very hard to estimate.

Even less is known—in fact, almost nothing—about the extent to which college graduates in some jobs are paid more *because* they are college graduates rather than because of additional productivity resulting from college training. And in the absence of careful studies, argument by anecdote and example reigns, with little basis for resolving extreme differences of viewpoint.

While the above considerations suggest some tendency for unadjusted earnings differentials to exaggerate the effects of formal education on productivity, the failure of market rates of pay to reflect the external economic benefits of new ideas suggests the possibility of substantial error in the opposite direction. The educational process is intimately related to advances in knowledge; and the importance of new knowledge to economic progress has long been recognized. (While the

---

[12] The two-percentage-point adjustment was reported in Becker's initial report on his research (*American Economic Review*, May 1960, p. 349). The rate-of-return estimate is from his book (pp. 79–88) and is slightly higher than his original estimate. References to most of the original studies of ability-education-earnings relationships are also in Becker's book, and some of the same references may be found in my *Economic Aspects of Education.*

link between new knowledge and economic gain is most obvious in the natural sciences and technology, similar links exist in other fields as well. To take but one example, advances in economic theory have increased our ability to avoid deep recessions, thereby raising real incomes substantially.) For a number of good reasons, the full economic benefits stemming from a new idea do not accrue to the individual (or group) who had the idea, and therefore earnings differentials fail to measure this part of the contribution of education to economic growth. Nor do earnings differentials reflect some of the other external economic benefits attributable to education: For instance, near-universal literacy facilitates the operation of a highly specialized exchange economy (in addition to enabling people to calculate their own income tax).[13]

It is easy to multiply examples of the above kind; it is, at the present state of our knowledge, impossible to make anything but the roughest kind of guess as to overall dollar value. All that is clear is that the dollar magnitude could be very large indeed.[14]

III. POLICY QUESTIONS

We turn now to a discussion of the applicability of the above type of analysis to such policy issues as the total amount to be invested in human capital and the allocation of costs between the private and public sectors.

The Amount to Be Invested in Human Capital. Is a large enough share of the country's total resources being devoted

[13] Burton A. Weisbrod has estimated that the annual value (as of 1960) of services performed by persons who filled out their own income tax returns amounted to about $66 million or almost 1 percent of all elementary school costs. ("Education and Investment in Human Capital," *Journal of Political Economy,* October 1962 Supplement, p. 115.)

[14] Becker calculates an upper limit to the true social rate of return by attributing all of Denison's "advancement-of-knowledge" residual to education; the results show social rates of return almost *double* the private rates. (See Chapter V of *Human Capital,* pp. 117–21.)

to investments in human capital? A rate-of-return approach can be very helpful in formulating an answer to this question, since it forces us to consider explicitly costs as well as benefits and to make comparisons among alternative courses of action. However, in interpreting the kinds of evidence on rates of return described in the previous section, there are a number of important considerations to be kept in mind.

First, the available estimates are, for reasons already noted, subject to a wide margin of error, and therefore must be regarded as suggesting orders of magnitude, not precise outcomes.

Second, the estimates are *average* rates of return on *past* investments, while for policy purposes we require estimates of the *marginal* rates of return that would be applicable to *new* investments. Some economists have argued, on law-of-diminishing-returns grounds, that additional investments must be expected to yield smaller returns than past investments. But this line of argument assumes that the demand side of the equation does not change—and there is no particular reason to think that this will be the case. In fact, available evidence contradicts the notion of an inexorable tendency for rates of return on education to decline as enrollment ratios rise. Between 1940 and 1960 the supply of educated persons in this country increased markedly, and yet the data do not indicate that rates of return on education have fallen.[15]

Whether dynamic factors will continue to operate in such a way as to maintain past rates of return is, of course, an open question, the answer to which will depend in large part on the character of future advancements in knowledge. Attempts have been made to forecast future demands for trained manpower of various kinds, but no great success can be (or has been) claimed. The relation between past and future

[15] See H. Miller, "Income in Relation to Education," *American Economic Review,* December 1960, p. 965; and Becker, "Underinvestment in College Education?", *American Economic Review* (*Papers and Proceedings*), May 1960, pp. 347–48, as well as his *Human Capital.*

rates of return will also depend on changes in the "mix" of the overall pool of investments in human capital. We know, for instance, that females earn a smaller economic return from college education than do males; therefore, if further increases in college enrollments were to occur mainly among the female population, the overall economic rate of return would be lower, other things equal, than if the increases were to occur mainly among males.

A third point is that rates of return on investments in human capital must be compared with other rates of return if an intelligent allocation of investment funds is to be made. Becker has used a before-tax rate of return on corporate manufacturing capital of 12 percent for comparative purposes and has concluded that, ignoring external effects, there is no presumption in favor of switching investment funds from the physical capital to the education category.[16] However, to the extent that one thinks that external benefits are likely to be greater in the case of human capital than physical capital, the case for stepping up investments in human capital relative to physical capital is strengthened accordingly.

When we think in terms of allocating a given pool of investment funds between the human and physical capital categories, it is well to remember that important complementarities probably exist. Education and research are the source of much new technological knowledge; this new knowledge must ordinarily be embodied in new machinery and equipment; and new machinery and equipment can be introduced more readily if the labor force possesses general knowledge and transferable skills.[17] Thus, to get the highest return from the total pool of investment funds it will be necessary to maintain the right proportions between human and physical capital and not treat the two types of investment as if they were unrelated.

[16] *Human Capital*, pp. 120–21.
[17] The economic case for general or "liberal" education rests heavily on the greater adaptability that this kind of education confers.

Nor should we overlook the very real possibility that it is in our best interest to increase our investments in *both* the physical and human capital categories—that is, the social rates of return on both types of investment may be high enough to justify further expenditures along both lines. This depends, of course, on society's preference for future, as opposed to present, consumption—a question discussed elsewhere in this volume.

Consideration number four is simply that the extent to which investments in human capital confer nonmonetary benefits on both the individuals in whom the investments are made, and on the society as a whole, must be taken into account in reaching policy decisions. The range of nonmonetary benefits accruing to the individual as a consequence of health and education expenditures is wide indeed. Perhaps most important is the pure pleasure of improved health. Education confers long-lasting benefits of the nonmonetary sort by awakening new interests and extending the range of activities which a person can enjoy in his leisure time. Mothers of elementary school children undoubtedly derive immediate pleasure from having their charges in school some of the time. And then there is the enjoyment by many students of the schooling process itself.[18] Furthermore, from the vantage point of society as a whole, it has long been recognized that education plays a vital role in the working of the democratic process.

The reason we must pay attention to benefits of this type in the context of a discussion of economic growth is that such benefits are obtained, for the most part, *simultaneously* with the training which enhances future economic productivity.

[18] This undoubtedly varies not only from student to student, but also with the stage of education. My armchair guess is that elementary school students as a group derive real pleasure from school, that in junior and senior high school feelings are much more mixed, and that in college the average degree of pleasure rises again, partly because we have considerable self-selectivity here—high school students who think they will like college are more apt to go than other students. At the graduate level, I would guess that the immediate pleasure component again fades more into the background.

That is, we are dealing with joint products; and there is no economically meaningful way of allocating many of the costs of education (or health care) so as to obtain separate monetary and nonmonetary rates of return. From a decision-making standpoint, this means that society must put a value on the nonmonetary benefits, add this value to the monetary benefits, and thus obtain a stream of total benefits which can be compared with total costs.[19]

Allocation of Costs Between the Public and Private Sectors. A second broad policy issue, not entirely divorced from the matter of total expenditure, has to do with assigning the responsibility of paying for health and education projects. The main economic question at issue here is: Can we rely on individuals, acting in their own self-interest, to invest the "right" amount (from the standpoint of society as a whole) in human capital?

Apart from social welfare and equality-of-opportunity considerations, there are two particular reasons for thinking that leaving education and health exclusively to the private sector would lead to an undesirably low rate of investment in human capital.

First, the existence of external ("social") benefits implies a need for government support, since all private individuals cannot be expected to include the full extent of community benefits in their own benefit/cost calculations. While comparatively few private individuals may think it worthwhile to finance basic research in biochemistry in the hope of decreasing the probability of their dying of cancer, such an investment may make very good sense from the standpoint of society as a whole. To take a second, even more obvious,

---

[19] The importance of looking at actual decisions in this way can be illustrated by considering the high school drop-out problem. The purely monetary returns to projects designed to reduce drop-outs are likely to be fairly low, as is indicated by a pilot study of a particular project carried out by Burton A. Weisbrod, "Preventing High School Dropouts," Robert Dorfman, ed., *Measuring Benefits of Government Investments*, Brookings Institution, 1965, pp. 117–71.

example from the health field, proper treatment of contagious diseases benefits many people besides those being treated. Still another type of external benefit is evident in the case of retraining programs—successful retraining reduces the costs to the community of unemployment compensation. At the elementary and secondary levels of education, the social benefits of elementary and high school education have been thought to be so great that attendance has been compulsory and direct costs have been paid from taxes.[20]

The second line of argument emphasizes "imperfections" in private capital markets and asserts that because of these imperfections some individuals will underinvest in themselves from a strictly private rates-of-return standpoint, let alone from a social rate of return perspective. Perhaps the main reason why individuals can be expected to have above-average difficulty in financing investments in human capital is that the slavery prohibition precludes giving the lender a claim to the asset itself. In addition, the pronounced dispersion in rates of return among individuals, and the long payoff period, mean that any single individual contemplating an investment in human capital faces considerable uncertainty; furthermore, many of these investments must be made at very young ages. Schools, with the aid of private philanthropists, have for years tried to alleviate these difficulties by providing scholarships and loans; and in recent years Federal Government loan and fellowship programs have been directed toward the same end.

Granted, then, that there is a case for *some* government support, the question remains: How far should the government go in meeting the costs of health and education pro-

---

[20] Actually, the benefits of elementary and high school education are not confined to the localities or even to the states in which the schooling occurs, but "spill over" to the country as a whole via the migration of educated people. This is one justification for federal government support. (See Burton A. Weisbrod, *External Benefits of Public Education*, Industrial Relations Section, Princeton University, 1964.)

grams? The answer will of course vary from program to program, depending on the balance between private and social benefit-cost ratios. Even in the case of a particular program, reasonable men will differ in their answers, partly because of differences in social values, and partly because there are open questions concerning the effects of various financing alternatives. For instance, in the case of higher education, to what extent would more reliance on loan finance deter able but impecunious children from pursuing their studies? Most economists are agreed that the fact that college students do receive significant private returns implies, on equity grounds, that students should pay at least a share of their own way. But having said this hardly closes the door on debate. To pursue the matter further would, however, take us too far afield.[21]

It would be nice to be able to end this essay by stating categorically what should and should not be done with regard to a long list of specific policy proposals. Unfortunately, this is not possible. To be sure, each of us is likely to have firmly held views on many of these policy questions. However, it would be wrong to claim that the current state of our knowledge permits us to prove very conclusively that the other fellow is wrong. What we have is an understanding of certain principles and a growing body of empirical information which together require that the economic effects of investments in human capital be taken seriously. And we also have tools of analysis which, when applied to concrete policy proposals, can at least suggest (roughly) the value which must be assigned to nonmonetary benefits if the proposal is to compare favorably with some given alternative use of the funds. While

[21] For a provocative discussion of the role of government in financing and directing education, see M. Friedman, "The Role of Government in Education," in Solo, ed., *Economics and the Public Interest*, Rutgers University Press, 1955. This subject, in the British context, is discussed at some length in the *Report of the Committee on Higher Education* [Robbins Committee], Cmnd. 2154, October 1963.

education and health are subjects which are characterized by strong expressions of personal viewpoints, it is becoming harder to reconcile any assertion with the evidence, and this is certainly a mark of progress.

Part VIII

Technological Advance, Economic Growth, and Public Policy

BY

Richard R. Nelson

The state of technological knowledge limits what can be done with labor, capital, and resources; what can be produced and how it can be produced.* The advance of technological knowledge, by opening new ways to meet wants, and by increasing the productivity of the nation's human and material resources, has been one of the most important factors contributing to the economic growth of the United States. It also has been a major source of economic disruption—destroying the value of old skills and assets as it creates demands for new ones. In this paper I shall first examine the role of technological change in the process of economic growth to provide a perspective on the benefits and costs involved. Then I shall discuss some of the problems and opportunities of public policy, with special emphasis given to policies with respect to research and development.

A. TECHNOLOGICAL ADVANCE AND ECONOMIC GROWTH

1. *Technological Advance and Economic Potential.* The advance of technological knowledge has increased the potential of the economic system to meet man's wants in several differ-

---

* Any views expressed in this paper are those of the author and should not be interpreted as reflecting the views of The RAND Corporation or the official opinion or policy of any of its governmental or private research sponsors. Papers are reproduced by The RAND Corporation as a courtesy to members of its staff.

ent ways. Sometimes improved technological knowledge has enabled a greater quantity of output to be produced from given inputs; thus the invention and adoption of the process of catalytic cracking greatly increased the amount of gasoline a given amount of labor and capital could produce from a barrel of crude oil. Sometimes technological advances have enabled the production of products better suited to certain wants; thus nylon fibers meet a wide variety of needs better than any natural fiber. And sometimes improved technological knowledge has enabled wants to be met which could not be met at all before: prior to the modern airplane it was impossible to travel across the country in less than two days, much less five hours—not more difficult or expensive—impossible.

Perhaps the most dramatic impact of technological change has been in the creation of new and potentially better ways to meet man's needs. The revolutionary improvements in health care which have increased life expectations from fifty years in 1900 to seventy years in 1960 could not have been achieved simply by allocating more men and equipment to health needs. This has happened, but the main factor which has permitted the improvement has been advance of medical knowledge and technique. The revolution in the ability to transport men and goods, and to communicate, likewise would have been impossible in the absence of the invention and development of the automobile, the airplane, and the radio.

In addition to expanding the range of possible goods and services, technological change has played an important role in increasing the productivity of capital and labor in the production of all kinds of goods. The output of steel that can be obtained from a given input of labor and capital has more than doubled since 1900. The same is true for productivity in the coal industry, in agriculture, in spinning of cotton yarn, and in most traditional industries. Compared with 1900, the American economy not only is capable of producing a wider and more satisfactory income of final products and services; it is capable of producing much more of all kinds of products.

In large part we have chosen to use our expanded overall economic potential in the production of new goods and services. But we could have chosen to do otherwise, and even without the improvements that have been achieved in the kinds of final products that can be produced, our increased productivity would have enabled a very substantial improvement in economic well-being. And even though we have not chosen to expand output greatly in some of the more traditional sectors, productivity gains in these sectors have played an important role in our economic growth. Thus, while we have not chosen to devote much of our increased economic potential to increased agricultural production, improvements in agricultural productivity have freed labor and capital for other uses (in particular, to produce new goods and services). Between 1950 and 1960, for example, one-quarter of the increase in the nonagricultural work force was comprised of people leaving the farm.

Unfortunately, there is no practical way of measuring the contribution to improved well-being of technological advance which results in really new goods and services. It is clear that the way our Gross National Product series is put together understates the contribution to economic well-being of this type of technological advance and there is no simple remedy for this accounting problem. However, the GNP series does account for productivity increases, and it is possible to get some qualitative feel for the role of technological change in this respect.

Roughly half of the growth of GNP experienced during the twentieth century can be explained by increases in labor and capital; and roughly half cannot. As the examples cited earlier suggest, over the economy as a whole since 1900 the output which a given amount of labor and capital can produce has more than doubled. While it is extremely difficult to isolate and quantify the contribution of the many factors which have generated this increased productivity, certainly improved technology is prominent among them.

There are only a few careful studies which have attempted to measure the productivity advances which have resulted from specific technological advances, but the results of these studies are quite impressive. For example, Enos' [1] study of the effects of various technological developments in catalytic cracking suggest productivity increases of several hundred percent. Griliches' [2] study of the effects of the introduction of hybrid corn also shows very great increases in productivity. The numerous histories of technology which have been written provide strong qualitative evidence of the tremendous impact upon productivity of various technological developments.

While these examples can provide a qualitative feel for the overall contribution of technological change, it is not possible to generalize from them quantitatively. Given the present state of our economic understanding, it simply is impossible to determine the overall contribution to economic growth which technological change has made; indeed, the contribution of advances in technological knowledge to the improved ability of the economic system to meet the material wants of society cannot be considered in isolation from the role of other factors.

Without substantial investment in education which increased the supply of highly trained scientists, engineers, and technicians, the pace of technological advance would have been significantly slower. To reap the benefits of new technology often required specialized materials, new capital equipment, and highly trained and educated manpower. And on the other hand, changes in the state of technological knowledge certainly played a role in determining trends in the terms on which the economy had access to various materials, the kinds of capital equipment that could be built and their

[1] John L. Enos, "Invention and Innovation in Petroleum Refining," *The Rate and Direction of Inventive Activity*, Princeton University Press, 1962.

[2] Zvi Griliches, "Research Costs and Social Returns: Hybrid Corn and Related Innovations," *Journal of Political Economy*, October 1958.

costs, and the type of technological information and patterns of technological thinking that were imparted to the students who became the nation's trained manpower. If technological advances had been less rapid, it would have been impossible to have achieved the growth of the capital stock we did achieve without sharply declining rates of profit on new physical investment; thus, the rate of growth of the capital stock probably would have been slower.

These examples only begin to suggest the interactions involved in the process of economic growth. But they are sufficient to explain why it is so difficult to isolate and quantify the role of technological change, or any other factor, in our past economic growth.

2. *Technological Change, Structural Adjustment, and Unemployment.* As was suggested in the previous section, beneath the changes in aggregative economic activity and performance there have been dramatic shifts in the composition of GNP and in the allocation of the nation's human and material resources. These changes in composition have been essential aspects of the process of economic growth and, in particular, of the way in which technological change affects the economic system. These shifts have permitted the society to gain maximum benefit from new technological advances. At the same time, however, the necessity of making these shifts has imposed serious social costs.

The changing composition of output and employment the United States has experienced since 1900 has been the result of interaction between changing patterns of demand and changing relative costs. It should be noted that even without technological advance there would have been a shift in the composition of output and employment. Per capita income would have grown significantly, tastes and values would have changed, capital would have grown more abundant relative to labor, and relative resource costs would have changed. All these factors would have stimulated changes in economic structure. However, it is difficult to avoid the judgment that, in the absence of technological change, the shift in the composition of output and employment would have been significantly smaller. Technological change certainly has played a major role both in shifting demand patterns (by changing the spectrum of products and services) and in changing relative costs (by creating new and more productive techniques). Rapid technological change is fundamentally disruptive.

Nor is the problem here that the market mechanism is reacting to the effects of technological change in a socially undesirable way. Shifting allocation of resources is an essential part of the process by which society takes maximum benefit from the new opportunities opened by technological advance. If an economy has freedom to reallocate its resources, it has a choice as to whether to take out the opportunities afforded by a technological breakthrough in one industry primarily in the form of increased output by that industry, or (by shifting labor from that industry to others) in the form of increased output by other industries. In general, when new and improved products have been developed, society has chosen to shift labor and resources to their production and away from production of close substitutes. When technological advance has led to increased efficiency in producing existing products, John Kendrick's[3] study has shown that the result in general has been lower prices and increased output of those products. In situations where price has been quite sensitive to cost reduction, and demand quite sensitive to changes in price, employment has increased. In situations where price has not been particularly sensitive to cost reductions or demand not particularly sensitive to price reductions, labor has been released. There are many examples of both cases and Kendrick's data show that instances of the former have been about as frequent as instances of the latter.

But regardless of whether employment expands or contracts in the industry experiencing technological change, in

[3] John Kendrick, *Productivity Trends in the United States*, Princeton University Press, 1961.

general, technological change has destroyed some jobs and created new ones. For many people it has been extremely difficult and painful to prepare for and find new jobs. The human costs, and ultimately they are the only costs which really matter, sometimes have been very high. This problem of structural adjustment is a serious one. It is a problem which would be with us even if technological change were significantly slower, but undoubtedly rapid technological changes intensify the problem. However, there is no evidence that the problem is more severe in recent years than it has been in the past.

Compared with other years of relatively high overall unemployment, there is no evidence that the past few years have been marked by increased concentration of unemployment either by age, by industry, or by location. The pattern of unemployment today is roughly what it has been in other periods of economic slack (in particular in 1949 and 1954); that is, relatively highly concentrated among the unskilled groups who are the last hired and the first fired, and in the industries that produce (directly or indirectly) capital goods. And history is clear that a good share of the problem in 1949 and 1954 was due to inadequate aggregate demand. When demand increased, both output and employment picked up smartly. The unemployed did not always return to the jobs they had left. But as the pressure of labor shortages grew, employers became more willing to train new people, and the structurally dislocated found it far easier to find new jobs.

It is clear that the problem of facilitating structural adjustment to technological change and the problem of keeping the overall level of aggregate demand roughly in equality with overall productive capacity are intimately related. In order to keep the human costs of technological change low, it is important that the nation have active programs to assure the flexibility and adaptability of the work force and to provide a living to those who, for one reason or another, are unable to acquire new jobs. It also is essential that fiscal and monetary policies be used effectively to keep aggregate demand growing in line with aggregate potential.

There is no intrinsic reason why increases in economic potential, no matter how fast, should not be matched by increases in demand. There is no reason to be afraid of the aggregate employment implications of rapid growth of productivity. Tobin's essay has suggested the range of private and public needs that increased economic potential could be used to meet. We, as a nation, must decide how we want to allocate our growing economic potential among these needs. Undoubtedly we want to allocate a portion to needs that can be met more efficiently through private spending, and a portion to needs that can be met most effectively through public spending. The balance between increased private and public purchasing power that will best meet our needs is a judgment which depends in large part on fundamental values and subjective judgments as to priorities. The decision with respect to this balance is rightly the subject of vigorous debate. But once a balance among competing national needs is determined through our political processes, it is the job of fiscal and monetary policy to try to assure that the total and pattern of effective demand actually calls forth the pattern of utilization of our human and material resources best suited to meet this schedule of needs. There is every reason to believe that we have the fiscal and monetary policy instruments and sufficient knowledge of how they affect demand, so that we can assure that increased economic potential is used to meet wants, and not frittered away in unemployment. But there is nothing automatic about this—to achieve it requires effective, courageous, and sensible policies. Above all it requires a citizenry that understands the problem.

With strong programs to deal with the problem of structural adjustment, and with effective fiscal and monetary policies to keep aggregate demand growing in line with aggregate potential, we can develop policies to increase the pace and improve the direction of technological advances with assurance that the gains will far exceed the costs.

B. PROBLEMS AND OPPORTUNITIES OF PUBLIC POLICY

1. *The Dimensions of Policy.* As was stressed in the previous section, it is extremely difficult to separate the effects of technological change from the effects of all the other factors which contribute to economic growth; it is even more difficult to delimit the set of policies which directly or indirectly affect the rate and direction of technological advance. Almost any policy which affects the rate of investment affects the rate at which new technology is introduced to the economic system, and the incentives for developing new technology. Policies with respect to education will affect strongly both the supply of people available to develop technology and the ability of management and labor to utilize that technology fruitfully. Effective programs of training and retraining labor, by reducing the human costs of technological process, may reduce the resistance to it.

Even if we consider only policies which are aimed directly at stimulating the development and use of new technology, the range of possible policies is very large. The process of technological change involves inventing, developing, testing, and applying new or improved ways of doing things. It involves dissemination of information and, perhaps most important of all, risk-taking and entrepreneurship. The institutions involved include research and development laboratories, libraries, trade and technical journals, industry and engineering societies, and the capital markets of the nation.

Policies with respect to technological advance must be concerned both with rate and direction at which the frontiers of technological knowledge advance, and with the extent to which actual practice keeps pace with the best that is known. The instruments of policy include the patent system, various incentives which can be built into the tax system, other laws and regulations, contracts, grants, and other forms of expenditures.

To cut down the discussion to manageable proportions in this paper I will deal only with one aspect of the policy problem—the role of federal policy in allocating scientific and technical resources, and particularly the allocation of resources among different kinds of Research and Development (R and D).

2. *R and D Allocation Makes a Difference.* For the purposes of this paper I will define R and D broadly as that activity which is directed toward advancing the frontiers of knowledge and will focus on R and D that creates knowledge of relevance in meeting man's wants through economic activity. The rate and direction of technological advance we can expect in the future will be strongly dependent upon the amount and allocation of resources devoted to R and D.

Often the discussion of the need for more R and D funds for one purpose or another tends to ignore the fact that the human and material resources which comprise our scientific and technical capability are scarce and valuable. Approximately 1.5 million scientists and engineers carry the major burden of the application and advancement of science and technology. The supply of these resources is not very elastic in the short run. If they are utilized in one job, they cannot be used in another.

As long as our scientific and technical resources are limited, we never shall be able to do all the things we want to do. These resources must be allocated between R and D and other uses. Only about one-third of the working time of the scientists and engineers of the United States is spent in R and D. Two-thirds is spent in teaching, management, and other functions. Over the long run, our scientific and technical capabilities will depend in large part on the number of new scientists and engineers provided by our education system, and thus we must face the policy problem of how large a share of our existing capabilities we should allocate to education, and how much to R and D and other functions. Over the short run, the speed with which industry picks up and uses efficiently the new products and processes developed by R and D depends in considerable part on the number of technically trained people in management, production engineering, sales, and technical communications. Thus, we must be concerned with the allocation of technically sophisticated people between R and D and these functions. But in this section the concern will be predominantly with the allocation of those resources involved in R and D, and only in small part with the allocation between R and D and other functions.

It is important how the resources involved in R and D as a whole are allocated among different kinds of R and D. Allocation makes a difference. While it is true that the areas of potential practical application of a basic research project are uncertain, that research on plastics can lead to better paints, and that the civilian economy sometimes can gain considerable benefit from the byproducts of military and space R and D, it is obvious that the particular R and D projects to which the talents of scientists and engineers are applied affects the types of payoffs society is most likely to get from their work. Perhaps the best evidence we have that the allocation of R and D really matters is provided by the Terleckyj[4] study which showed that there has been a significant correlation between R and D spending (and the scientists and engineers employed by an industry) and the rate of growth of productivity in that industry. While the historical record shows that many of the most significant technical advances affecting the productivity of an industry originate from research done in other industries, or in university or government laboratories,

[4] Nestor Terleckyj, "Sources of Productivity Change," unpub. doctoral dissertation, Columbia University, 1959. In Kendrick, *op. cit.*, p. 183.

it is apparent that research done by the industry itself is important.

For the technology of a particular sector or industry to be advanced with any speed and regularity requires that competent and imaginative people be working specifically to that end. While very often technological advances in one use have application in another, it generally requires technically competent people to see this and it often requires some modification and adaptation. While often many of the technological problems of several industries or sectors are similar, often many of the problems are quite different and require specialized attention and treatment. In short, the allocation of resources to R and D among different industries, and for different purposes, has a definite effect on the kinds of technological advances we can expect.

At the present time, Research and Development in the United States is highly concentrated on a few important areas of demand or need. Of the R and D done in industry (about 70 percent of the nation's total R and D effort), over 60 percent is financed by the Department of Defense or NASA and aimed at developing equipment or knowledge for their purposes. This is reflected in the fact that more than 55 percent of industrial R and D is performed by two related industry groups—the aircraft missiles and parts industry, and the electrical equipment and communication industry. The chemical industry, motor vehicles and other transportation equipment industry, and the machinery industry perform most of the rest. The concentration is no less when account is taken of the product fields to which the research is directed. Further, most of the work is done in a few firms. In 1960, over 85 percent of R and D was done by the industrial grants of the economy; firms employing 5,000 or more people.

However, it must be recognized that not all of the efforts aimed at inventing and developing new technology are counted in the R and D statistics, or even are done by scientists and engineers. For example, in 1953, over 60 percent of patents resulted from the work of part-time or private inventors; and history suggests that the work of private and part-time inventors often is quite significant. It also must be recognized both that industry lines can be deceptive—the chemical industry produces textile fibers—and that often the technology of an industry is advanced through the R and D of material and equipment suppliers. For these reasons, the R and D allocation statistics can give some misleading impressions. But in any case, clearly the notion that a considerable amount of Research and Development is being directed to almost all sectors of the economy is fallacious. Only a small amount of R and D is being directed, for example, at problems of developing urban mass-transport systems or improved materials, designs, or construction techniques for houses.

Of course, concentration of the nation's R and D effort is far from sufficient evidence that significant improvements in allocation are possible. In the first place, the importance of improving the performance and quality of products or services is greater in certain fields than in others: Clearly the costs of having a potential enemy drastically outstrip us in performance of military equipment are so great that sufficient R and D must be allocated to defense purposes to assure that this will not happen. Improvements in the field of medicine also clearly are of great importance. Second, the potential gains from increasing productivity are greater in some fields than in others; in general, the greater the quantity of human and material resources used in an industry, the greater the potential gains to society of a given percentage increase in productivity. These gains from resources saved can be realized in the industry where the productivity advances occur, or the gains can be used to permit the transfer of resources to other industries. Third, technological promise certainly is greater in some fields than in others; thus it may be that R and D aimed at increasing agricultural productivity is more likely to yield significant advances than R and D aimed at increasing efficiency in housing construction. And, to repeat, the gains in increases in agricultural productivity can be used to permit an increase in the quantity of labor and capital allocated to meeting the housing needs of the nation.

Thus, the fact that resources are very unevenly distributed over different fields in itself provides no clue regarding diversion from optimality. Nor does the fact that some or even a considerable amount of R and D is going on in a particular field demonstrate that enough is going on. The relevant question is whether or not it is possible to shift the allocation of R and D resources so as to improve the relevance of R and D output to the needs of the nation.

The answer to this question probably is yes. The reason is that, in the absence of public policies, there is nothing automatic about the system of incentives and institutions allocating R and D resources which generates an optimal allocation. And the need for active public policy to assure an optimal allocation has not generally been recognized.

3. *The Role of Public Policy.* One of the major tasks of public formulation is to decide which areas of Research and Development are likely to receive adequate support from nongovernmental organizations, and which areas are not likely to be adequately supported. Where the public interest is reasonably well reflected in private profit opportunities and private capabilities exist, we can rely on private groups to do the job. In those areas where the benefits of R and D are not adequately reflected in private incentives or capabilities, it is the task of public policy either to increase private incentives or capabilities, or to get the job done through public agencies.

Traditionally, with a few important exceptions, the United States has relied heavily on the workings of the market and on private initiative to generate the R and D designed to advance civilian technology. And for stimulating R and D on product improvement and new product development in sectors where there is a well-working market, this probably is the most sensible thing to do. A business firm, feeling the needs of the economy as expressed through the market, and stimulated to meet these needs by the lure of profit and the spur of competition, can engage in this kind of R and D reasonably sure that, if successful, it will be well rewarded. The knowledge created by this type of work is likely to be directly relevant to the firm's problems. The firm is likely to be able to make private property of the new technology through a suitably written patent. And this patent is quite likely to enable the firm to share in any economic benefits created by the knowledge for activities outside the range of the firm's market interests. For this type of R and D, in most instances, the public interest probably is quite adequately reflected in private incentives and met by private capabilities.

At the same time, the Federal Government traditionally has had a direct responsibility for seeing to it that for those areas of the political economy where there is *not* a well-working market, the investment in R and D is of adequate size and quality, given the returns and the costs. While programs related to national security dwarf quantitatively the other governmental R and D programs, which are conducted out of a responsibility to manage efficiently a "public function," there are many other areas as well. The Government has a recognized major responsibility for supporting research to improve weather forecasting, public health, and public roads, to name just a few. This does not mean that the Government must do all of the work in its own facilities or that it must finance all, or any, of the work. But because, in the absence of specific policies, there is no effective market generating private incentives to provide the goods and services involved (this is why public agencies have direct responsibility in the first place), the Government has an implied responsibility for seeing that the appropriate R and D is done, in one way or another.

At these two extremes, the division of responsibility is widely recognized. But recognition of public responsibility is one thing and development of effective policy is another and, as will be discussed later, in several fields public policy falls short of recognized public responsibility. Further, between the clear-cut public and private domains there exists a large and important middle ground where it is clear the market works very poorly, and where as yet no clear-cut public responsibility has been established.

Our enterprise system tends to work poorly in situations where one company takes the risks and covers the costs but many companies share widely in the benefits. The whole area of process improvements not subject to patenting (a major source of productivity growth), of testing and evaluation techniques, and of analysis of materials and methods, are cases in point. The results often do not result in a patentable invention, and have widespread potential use. Research on standards, and on user safety, is also unlikely to yield a private firm profits commensurate with the benefits to society.

This problem is particularly serious for research and experimental development exploring advanced concepts and designs. This work is risky—in most cases the knowledge created will not be sufficient in itself to permit the design of a marketable product or process, but rather will suggest additional R and D, or may prove a blind alley. Often the information created may be of as much relevance to another company's problems as to those of the company sponsoring the research. In all save the largest and most secure firms, the time horizons are too short and the possibilities of spreading the risk too limited to give a firm strong incentive to do much of this kind of work. But society's interests are very long-run, and for society as a whole risks are spread over a very large number of projects.

Another problem area is R and D which cuts across the market interests of several firms. For example, the analysis of and development of integrated production systems is not easily forthcoming where there is no equipment supplier who produces a full range of equipment for a particular production sequence.

All of these problems are likely to be particularly serious

in industries comprised principally of small firms. Small firms often find too little use for highly trained engineers to hire them and often are unable to attract and hold them even when an effort is made. They thereby tend to be cut off from keeping up with the innovations of others as well as from innovating themselves.

As a result of these problems, it is likely that the present allocation of R and D resources in the United States is far from optimal. It probably diverges from optimality in at least three respects.

First, aside from the fields of defense and space, peacetime atomic energy, and perhaps public health, it is likely that we are relying too much on private incentives as stimulated by the market to generate R and D relevant to the public sector. Very little is being spent, for example, in research to improve urban transportation systems or educational technology. While it is not obvious that more research in these areas would yield considerable results, it is clear that the Government is only beginning to look into the question carefully. But if the Government does not take responsibility in these areas, no one else will. The Bureau of the Budget and the federal Council for Science and Technology should, each year, be responsible for evaluating the quantity and quality of research going on that is relevant to the needs of the public sector.

Second, aside from the fields of defense and space, there probably is too little research and experimentation aimed at exploring radically new techniques and ways of meeting needs. While it is true that this type of R and D need not be aimed specifically at a particular need in order to have considerable relevance to it, surely we can do better than to rely so heavily on "spill-over" from defense and space to open up the really new possibilities in materials, energy sources, etc. Since this kind of R and D is very risky, the benefits difficult to appropriate, and often relatively expensive, better mechanisms should be worked out so that industry can support such work cooperatively, and perhaps in financial partnership with the

Federal Government. These same comments also apply to process research and research on standards and materials.

Third, many industries and sectors presently are doing very little R and D because of the traditions and styles of management, because the firms are small relative to the size needed to support an efficient R and D effort, or because the perceived range of market interests and competence is too narrow to justify the support of anything but quite mundane R and D. In large part, the problem here can only be solved by broadening the perspectives of management and by infusing more engineering talent into the firms of the industry so that they can recognize and seize new opportunities. But various techniques of research support and cooperation, supplemented by a vigorous program of technical education and communication, could stimulate the sectors involved to expand their perspectives and technological sophistication.

As was indicated earlier, there are a wide variety of policy instruments and institutional arrangements which can be used to deal with these three problem areas. The U.S. experience with policies in support of technological change in agriculture and aviation is rich with techniques which might be tried elsewhere. Many foreign nations have developed various programs from which we can learn. But it must be acknowledged frankly that we presently do not know enough to predict with confidence what the most successful approaches will be.

It also must be recognized that a developing policy to stimulate more and better directed R and D is only one part of overall growth policy. Indeed, it is only one part of policy with respect to the stimulation of technological advance. In many instances, the applicable results of past R and D simply are not being applied, and policies to educate potential users and to remove obstacles to the use of existing technology probably have a much higher rate of return than policies to accelerate the rate at which the frontiers of knowledge are being advanced. In many cases, the gains from more R and D would be negligible unless complementary actions are taken to facilitate and stimulate the use of the results. A developing program of stimulus of R and D must be viewed in this broader context. Specific policies of research support must be weighed against a wide spectrum of alternatives, and fitted into a coherent package with other policies which affect technological advance and economic growth. And the developing program of stimulas of R and D should be pragmatic, experimental, and flexible, so that we can learn as we go along.

Part IX

Fixed Investment and Economic Growth

Robert M. Solow

In economics, as in more exact sciences, it sometimes happens that progress comes from exploiting the implications of rather simple insights or observations. The original observation itself may be nothing new; what counts is the realization that it is the key to something else. Thus, much of the modern analysis of economic growth begins from the simple truism emphasized by Sir Roy Harrod and by Evsey Domar: Investment in plant and equipment differs from other possible uses of output in an important way. Investment adds both to current demand for output and to future capacity to produce output. Consumption and military expenditures, on the other hand, may be important sources of demand for current output, but they do not add to capacity.

From a short-run point of view it hardly matters whether an increment to this year's national product takes the form of consumption or investment. It matters to the particular firms that make the sales and the particular workers and places affected. But it matters much less to the economy as a whole. From a longer-run point of view, however, it matters quite a lot. There is an optimistic way and a pessimistic way to state the difference. If the extra expenditures are investment, next year the economy will be able to produce more; it will have grown. That is the optimistic side. But if the economy is having trouble generating enough demand to employ its people and resources fully, then next year it will have an even harder problem if it invests this year, because still more demand will be needed to achieve full employment than if the investment had not taken place. That is the pessimistic view. Which view is more appropriate depends on circumstances. An economy which has been growing smoothly at full employment can "choose" confidently between slightly faster and slightly slower growth. An economy beset by unemployment and slack must be more cautious about the hurdles it sets for itself.

This approach dovetails perfectly with what has come to be called "the new economics" (though to professional economists it is thoroughly middle-aged). The analytical foundation of the Kennedy-Johnson economic policy was the proposition that the appropriate indicator for policy needs is the relationship between the potential output of the economy and the current state of demand, the Gap. When the Gap is large, when demand and production fall short of potential, there is room— and need—for expansionary policy, even if production is already rising. When the Gap is narrow or nonexistent, rapid expansion of demand will waste itself in inflation, because production can advance no more rapidly than potential output rises. If the democratic process suggests that more rapid growth is desirable, then the appropriate goal for policy is to shift some resources from current consumption to investment, to build capacity for the future, as discussed by James Tobin. The tension between demand and capacity, crucial for short-term policy decisions, is also the thing to watch when it comes to long-run economic growth.

Changes in national product can be decomposed into changes in potential output and changes in unemployment and capacity utilization. From year to year, changes in unemployment and the rate of capacity utilization can be the dominant source of changes in national product. But over long periods of time, barring major economic collapse, the change in potential must dominate. If a twenty-year period begins with a Gap of 10 percent and ends with none at all, then Gap-closing contributes something under 0.5 percent a year to the rate of growth of production. For the United States, the long-period growth of potential output has been something between 3 and 4 percent a year. So it is clear that when we turn attention to growth over several decades, the recorded growth of the economy *is*, to a good approximation, the growth of potential output.

INVESTMENT AND POTENTIAL OUTPUT

The effect of investment on potential output can be separated into three components. Without a heavy burden of extra assumptions, it is a terribly difficult matter to measure the three component effects of investment, but nevertheless it pays to keep them separate for clarity of thought. The first effect is usually called "capital-widening" by economists. When employment is growing, the stock of plant and equipment must grow at the same rate simply to provide each of the new workers with the same amount of capital on the average as those already at work. A simplified numerical example—with numbers of about the right size—will help to explain this. Suppose that 70 million people are employed this year, and employment will grow by about 1.5 percent to 71 million next year. If each worker, on the average, is equipped with $20,000 worth of plant and machinery, $20 billion of net investment is required to outfit the new workers up to the standard of the old. If production per man is about $10,000, the national product amounts to $700 billion; the "capital-widening" investment is a bit under 3 percent of the national product.

In the course of time, however, the amount of capital per worker goes up. Even if invention did not generate new processes of production using new kinds of equipment, it would be possible (and might be profitable) to provide more of already known types of capital for each worker. There are always a few more ways to increase productivity per worker: mechanize materials-handling, for example, or replace hand-mixed concrete by machine-mixed. This process is often called "capital-deepening." Suppose—in the numerical example already mentioned—capital per worker were rising ("being deepened") by about 2 percent a year, from $20,000 to $20,400, for instance. Then the net investment required to bring all 71 million workers up to the new standard would be $400 × 71,000,000 or about $28.5 billion, another 4 percent of the national product.

A certain amount of capital-deepening does go on all the time. But invention rarely stands still. The hypothetical process of providing *more* capital per worker is inextricably mixed up with the theoretically different process of providing *better* capital for each worker. This aspect of investment has no such conventional name as the others. I once called it "capital-quickening," for the following reason. Plant and equipment has a fairly long life. It takes a while to wear out; and even if more efficient types of plant and equipment are invented every year, it takes a while before an older type becomes truly obsolete. This means that the stock of capital goods in an economy represents many "layers" of technology—old, not-so-old, and relatively new. The more investment occurs this year, the newer or younger, on the average, will be the stock of capital goods. In fact, the more investment occurs this year, the more old capital will be forced into idleness or out of existence by the competition of newer, more efficient capacity. Since new capital is generally more productive than old, a higher rate of investment has an additional productivity-increasing effect. This "quickening" effect can, in principle, be measured, even though one can not hope to isolate a particular dollar sum of new plant and equipment and identify it as the quickening part of total investment.

These three effects are worth distinguishing because they explain something about the effects of investment and about the motives for investment. Widening increases capacity without increasing productivity per worker. Deepening and quickening increase capacity by increasing productivity, but they do it differently. When more capital is provided per worker, there is likely to be pressure on profits, because the more profitable uses of capital are likely to be tried first. This is an application of the famous "law of diminishing returns." But when better capital is provided for some workers, there need be no weakening of profitability. Invention is the historical answer to the law of diminishing returns.

In principle, any expenditure or use of resources is an investment if it will yield a return in the future. Evidently, then, plant and equipment spending is investment spending, but so are some other types of expenditure. In particular, research and development expenditures are investment, and so is at least some—perhaps most—spending on education. These "intangible" kinds of investment are discussed at length in the papers by Bowen and Nelson; in this essay, investment means "plant and equipment spending." The one-word description is used, not with imperialistic intent, simply to avoid circumlocution. Casual observation as well as some more systematic evidence suggest that productivity can increase solely as a result of intangible investment. Nevertheless, it is fair to say that any commitment to economic growth involves, sooner or later, a commitment to investment in plant and equipment. Investment in that narrow sense may not be a sufficient condition for rapid growth, but it is almost certainly a necessary condition.

INTERNATIONAL COMPARISONS

Some evidence for this assertion comes from international comparisons. There is no doubt at all that, generally speaking, fast-growing countries are high-investment countries. Table 1 gives a sample of the evidence. Table 2 covers fewer countries for a more recent period. The first column gives the rate of growth of productivity, *i.e.*, of output per man-hour, not of output itself. The part of output growth that just reflects the growth of population and employment is excluded as not specially interesting. The second column shows for each country the proportion of Gross National Product devoted to gross investment (including inventories but excluding housing) on the average between 1950 and 1960. The third column is a crude experiment. Since the growth of employment has been eliminated from the first column by concentrating on productivity, it is natural to exclude from investment the part that constitutes capital-widening. Unfortunately, the third column is sheer guess; indeed, it is not even that, but a rule of thumb applied indiscriminately to all countries.

TABLE 1

	(1) Rate of Growth of Output per Man- hour, Annual Average 1950–60	(2) Proportion of GNP Invested, Annual Average 1950–60	(3) "Nonwidening" Investment as Proportion of GNP
Belgium	2.5	12.1	11.5
Denmark	2.9	15.3	14.5
France	3.9	15.3	14.3
Germany	6.0	19.0	15.8
Italy	4.1	16.1	12.5
Netherlands	3.7	20.0	17.8
Norway	3.9	23.0	24.0
Sweden	3.5	16.3	16.7
United Kingdom	2.0	12.1	10.9
Canada	2.5	20.1	17.5
United States	2.4	14.6	12.8

Source: Angus Maddison, *Economic Growth in the West*, The Twentieth Century Fund, New York, 1964.

Table 1 shows that the very fast-growing economies—West Germany, Norway, and Japan, for instance—did a lot of investment, more than most others. The very slow-growing economies—especially the United States and the United Kingdom—did much less investment than anyone else. But Table 1 also shows that no simple generalization will quite describe the facts, because once the extreme cases are set aside, the connection between growth of productivity and investment is loose. France has invested rather less, Norway and Canada rather more than their growth rates might lead one to expect. The tremendous increase in German productivity from 1950 to 1960 undoubtedly contained a nonrepeatable element of recovery from war. Table 2 gives a fairer picture. Indeed,

TABLE 2

	Rate of Growth of Output per Man, Annual Average 1955–64	Proportion of GNP Invested, Annual Average, 1955–64	"Nonwidening" Investment as Proportion of GNP
France	4.7	15.7	15.1
Germany	4.4	20.1	17.5
Italy	5.7	16.9	16.8
Japan	8.8	30.2	27.2
United Kingdom	2.6	13.7	12.7
United States	1.9	13.9	11.5

Source: Angus Maddison in *Lloyds Bank Review,* January 1966.

more detailed research has indicated that fast-growing countries grow fast as much because their investment is more productive as because they invest more in the first place. Some of this is easily understood: Cold countries like Norway and large, sparsely populated countries like Canada use up a lot of capital simply overcoming weather and distance. But it is not all so obvious. Some students of the problem have emphasized that the causal arrow points both ways: High investment may contribute to growth, but growth—especially uninterrupted growth—both motivates investment and permits more productive, less defensive, investment.

EVIDENCE FROM AMERICAN HISTORY

It is not necessary to go outside the United States to find evidence of this kind. Different periods of our own history can be used as the raw material for similar comparisons. The advantage of this procedure is that it avoids the vague implication that one country is pretty much like another except in those respects explicitly mentioned in Tables 1 and 2. We know that is not so. Table 2 must not be read as saying that if the British would only invest as large a fraction of their national income as the Japanese, they could grow as rapidly. The truth is that there is probably nothing the British economy could do that would make it grow as fast as the Japanese; the two countries differ in natural resources, social structure, attitudes, industrial composition, the scope for imitation and the willingness to imitate, and all sorts of things. When we deal with different slices of American history, many of these unmeasured and unmeasurable factors are constant or changing only slowly. The disadvantage of this historical procedure is that we need to compare fairly long periods—so that changes in potential dominate changes in output—and good statistics do not go back very far.

The periods from 1929–47 and from 1947–65 are comparable and fairly long. The end points were years of fairly high employment, so rates of growth are not much distorted by Gap-opening and Gap-closing. Between 1929 and 1947, the stock of plant and equipment (in constant prices) increased only about as fast as the number of people employed. Capital was widened, but not deepened. Moreover, the 1947 stock of capital was certainly older on the average than the 1929 stock; there was no gain in productivity from that source. There is no mystery about this; the period spans the deep depression of the 1930's, when very little investment occurred because very few opportunities for profit presented themselves, and the Second World War, when civilian investment was severely restricted. But we are interested in effects, not causes. Between 1929 and 1947, output per worker in American industry rose at the relatively slow rate of 1.5 percent a year. We can attribute this productivity gain mainly to technological progress, to the improved education and training of workers, and perhaps to other, minor, sources. That productivity rose at all between 1929 and 1947 shows that productivity can rise without much investment. That productivity rose so slowly suggests that without much investment there can not be very rapid progress.

Between 1947 and 1965, the stock of capital goods increased much more rapidly than employment. High investment increased the stock of plant and equipment per worker by something near 3 percent a year. During the same interval, production per worker also rose by nearly 3 percent a year. It would be too simple-minded to compare the prewar and postwar histories and conclude that capital-deepening at a rate of 3 percent a year generates a growth in productivity of about 1.5 percent a year (the 3 percent observed in 1947–65 less the 1.5 percent observed without deepening in 1929–47). One would have to pay more attention to changes in the hours of work, in the "quality" of the labor force, and in the industrial composition of the national product. One would have to attribute some gain in productivity to the fact that the 1965 stock of capital was a few years younger, on average, than the 1947 stock. Still, when all is said and done, it is hard to dodge the implication that the recovery of plant and equipment spending after the doldrums of depression and the rationing of wartime had quite a lot to do with the accelerated growth of productivity.

The same sort of correlation between investment and productivity gain is revealed by the comparison of shorter intervals of time. But the meaning of the correlation is much less clear. The productivity movements may have more to do with fluctuations in capacity utilization than with anything else. And the correlation may simply reflect the fact that rapid growth in output eliminates excess capacity and stimulates investment. That cannot be the mechanism underlying the longer-period comparisons.

THE "NATURAL" RATE OF GROWTH

Here I must deal with a fine point. Modern economic theory suggests that in the very long run the rate of economic growth is approximately the rate of growth of the labor force plus something that might be broadly identified as the rate of increase of economic efficiency. This last catchall is meant to include the rate of technological progress, the increase in output resulting from changes in industrial composition, movements from low-productivity to high-productivity activity, gains from the elimination of discrimination in employment, and many other things. The most important is technological progress. Another important component, stemming from the improvement in quality of the labor force, through more and better education and better health, can be included either as part of the growth of the labor force or as part of the increase of economic efficiency, so long as it is included somewhere. Barring the appearance of a growing Gap, the rate of economic growth will not in the very long run fall short of this "natural" rate of growth. Neither can it for very long be greater.

This implies that for the very long run the rate of growth does not depend on the rate of investment. It implies, roughly speaking, that the only way to create a permanent increase in the rate of growth is somehow to speed up the rate of technological progress. The reasoning behind this conclusion is complicated, but it goes something like this. If an economy that has been growing at its "natural" rate tries to grow faster by investing, say, 15 percent of its output instead of 10 percent, it will at first succeed in doing so. It will supply each worker with more capital and so enable each worker to produce more. The higher output means a higher rate of growth. On the average, too, each worker will have newer capital, and this will add to productivity and growth. But then the law of diminishing returns sets in. Each successive addition to capital per man is able to generate only successively smaller increases in productivity. And as the increments to output get smaller, so do the increments to capital, because investment remains a steady percentage of output. There is a permanent gain in production; that is very important to remember. An economy investing 15 percent of its annual income will forever after have a higher annual income than if it had continued to invest 10 percent. But eventually the gain tapers off. Suppose it tapers off at 20 percent; that is, eventually the economy will have a 20 percent higher output when it invests 15 percent than it would if it had continued to save 10 percent. At the end of twenty years, the economy will have added something under 1 percent a year to its growth rate; but at the end of fifty years, its growth rate will be only 0.4 percent higher than it would have been; and after a century, only 0.2 percent higher. These are not necessarily realistic numbers, but they illustrate the point. The very long-run growth rate may be determined by more fundamental forces than the rate of investment in plant and equipment. But the very long run may be very long. There may be quite respectable increases in the rate of growth achievable over spans of a decade or two. For an economy growing at 4 percent a year, the addition of a half a percentage point to the growth rate is no mean achievement. The sort of achievement it is can be best understood in connection with Tobin's paper in this volume.

It appears, then, that meaningful increases in economic growth can result either from higher investment or faster invention. Moreover, there are many subtle interconnections between the two. Some inventions are no use without investment; investment often stimulates invention. If necessity is the mother of invention, investment may well serve as midwife.

This excursion into theory provides us with an understanding of the looseness of the relation between investment and growth revealed in Table 1. Some part—it is no casual matter to say how much—of international differences in growth rates reflects differences in "natural" rates of growth: in the rate of innovation or imitation, in the rate at which the efficiency of use of existing resources under existing technology is being improved, in the rate at which the education and training of the labor force is being upgraded. Some part, of course, does reflect differences in the rate of investment. If the analysis I have mentioned is right, this part is in a very long-run sense transitory. But in the medium run it is quite real; and the investment rate differs from the other determinants of growth by being more easily and quickly changeable through the influence of public policy. It is also more directly a mere instrument. Society does or may have an intrinsic interest in education for its own sake, in innovation for its own sake, in the movement of people for their own sake out of low-productivity agriculture into high-productivity industry, but investment in plant and equipment has no reason for being other than the generation of new capacity. If investment were not necessary for economic growth, it would surely be better to produce consumer goods instead.

FUTURE INVESTMENT
REQUIREMENTS

The next question follows naturally. Suppose the United States were to grow for the next ten years as its natural rate: About how much plant and equipment investment would be required? And how much extra investment would be needed as part of a policy to speed the rate of growth a little?

Only the most uncertain sort of answer can be given. We do not even know for sure what the natural rate of growth is: The Council of Economic Advisers estimates 3.75 percent a year, with the possibility that some speed-up has taken place, while the National Industrial Conference Board, in a recent study, settles on a figure near 4.25 percent a year for the decade to 1975. Even if we take a round number like 4 percent as a compromise, there remain uncertainties. Something depends on how much of the 4-percent growth represents increase in employment, and how much represents increased productivity. Employment growth must be accompanied by capital-widening; productivity growth comes in part, but only in part, from capital-deepening. Another uncertainty has to do with the character of technological progress. Some students of the problem believe that there has been, in the past decade or more, a reduction in capital requirements per unit of national product. If this saving of capital is projected into the future, the investment requirements for any given rate of growth are reduced. Others prefer not to project a decline in capital requirements, either because they do not believe it has occurred or because they believe it to be temporary. They do not foresee any independent reduction in investment requirements from that source.

With all due caution, it is probably fair to say that most estimates of the fixed investment necessary to support 4 percent growth for a decade would cluster around 10 percent of GNP, some a little higher, others a little lower. Is that a lot of investment or a little? The easiest way to answer is to say that since the end of the Second World War the American economy has spent roughly 9 percent of its GNP on plant and equipment. The figure has dipped to 8.5 percent in bad years, and has risen to 10 percent or better only in 1947 and 1948, again in 1956 and 1957, and again in 1965–67 and, according to most forecasts, in 1968. The investment requirements of 4-percent growth are likely to be met by our economy in good years, and missed by 1 percent of GNP—which is 10 percent of the required investment—in slack years.

Now suppose it were desired to raise the growth rate to 4.25 percent: By how much would investment requirements rise? The difference between 4- and 4.25-percent growth sounds almost trivial, but it is not; it amounts to 2.5 percent of GNP in the tenth year alone, or between $15 and $20 billion at current levels. Now there are many ways of adding a little to the growth rate: working longer hours, inducing more women or old people into employment, speeding up the rate of migration from agriculture, to name a few. To do it all by increasing the rate of investment means fighting harder against diminishing returns, and that may be expensive. It would not be easy to get agreement on the magnitudes involved; much of the necessary research has not yet been done. But I suppose that to add 0.25 percent to the "natural" growth rate and sustain it for a decade would require fixed investment to rise above 12 percent of GNP; some might say well above 12 percent of GNP. That is very high by historical standards in this country. It would undoubtedly require special policies to stimulate investment. And not simply to induce business to more of the kind of investment it had been doing. To "deepen capital," to work against diminishing returns, means to encounter less profitable opportunities for investment. Policy must overcome this drag.

INVESTMENT AS DEMAND

From consideration of the capacity-creating effect of investment, logic has returned us to consideration of investment as a component of aggregate demand.

Directly or indirectly, all incomes are earned in production. The national income and the national product are opposite sides of the same coin. Moreover, earners of income spend to buy back the product they have collectively produced. It is possible for changes in inventories to absorb short-run fluctuations in spending; but over any substantial period of time, total expenditures and total production must move together. If spending falls off, production will drop too. But then incomes will fall and spending will drop still further, and then . . . these are the "multiplier effects" that every schoolboy knows, now.

At full employment—however that is defined—the economy

can produce a certain volume of output; in so doing it generates the corresponding total of incomes. Full employment will be maintainable only if the recipients of income are collectively willing to buy back the full-employment output. It seems, then, that they are required to spend all that they earn. Many people and many corporations, however, spend less than they earn; they save. Somewhere in the economic system, then, there must be someone or some institution prepared willingly to spend more than it earns. Otherwise the initial level of output and employment will be unmaintainable.

Imagine the economy grouped into three big consolidated sectors: families, businesses, and governments. Families earn wages, rents, dividends, salaries, and buy consumer goods. Businesses retain some part of their profits, accumulate depreciation allowances, and buy plant and equipment. Governments collect taxes from families and businesses and buy all the various things governments do buy. Typically, all families taken together spend considerably less than they earn, saving the difference. Typically, governments spend somewhat more than they take in—they run budget deficits—but, except in wartime the difference is small and there are many more surplus years than the mythology suggests. Businesses together spend on investment considerably more than they retain in undistributed profits and depreciation allowances; they run a big deficit. In 1965 the saving of households amounted to $25 billion and the saving (budget surplus) of governments to $2 billion. Against this, the gross saving of businesses was about $82 billion and their gross investment $109 billion. The $27 billion of saving by families and governments was offset by the excess of investment over retained earnings and depreciation allowances of business. (In these figures gross investment includes house-building, inventory accumulation, and net foreign investment in addition to plant and equipment spending; and a certain amount of personal saving is really the "business saving" of unincorporated businesses. But the principle is clear.)

Full employment can be maintained only if business and government together have a big enough deficit (or surplus) to offset the saving (or overspending) that families will do from the incomes they earn at full employment. (Personal saving has been positive every year since 1929 except for 1932 and 1933; at full employment it would certainly be positive.) If we freeze the consolidated budget deficit of all governments at zero or any convenient positive or negative number, this means that investment spending must be big enough to absorb the gross saving of business and the net saving of families. If it is not big enough to do so, markets are not strong enough to buy up the full-employment output of the economy; production, employment, and income will shrink to squeeze out the excess saving. If investment is bigger than it need be, aggregate expenditure will exceed the value of production at the going prices; prices and production will both rise, but the nearer the economy is to capacity operation, the more the excess demand will waste itself in inflation.

ECONOMIC POLICY

Economic policy in this context—there are many other goals of economic policy—has two objectives. Above all, the fiscal —tax and budget—and monetary policy of the Federal Government should aim to balance the economy at full employment. This can be accomplished by influencing the spending decisions of private families and businesses, and therefore their net saving. It can also be accomplished by operating on tax rates and government spending, and therefore on the net saving of governments. In fact, both devices will always be used. The immediate purpose is to guarantee that total expenditure from full-employment income is just enough to buy full-employment output, or that total investment should just offset total saving at full employment; these are two ways of saying the same thing.

This objective of economic policy can be achieved, in principle, by many combined fiscal-monetary strategies. The full-employment objective bears primarily on the total of expenditures, not on the way the total is divided among the three major sectors of consumption, investment, and government purchases. Of course, the allocation of total production can not be haphazard; it must conform roughly to the pre-existing distribution of industrial capacity, which can itself be changed only slowly. There is much evidence, for example, that the sharp capital-goods boom of 1956–57 strained the capacity of the equipment-producing industries with inflationary consequences for the whole economy. Despite this limitation, it remains true that there can be full employment with a broad range of "mixes" of personal consumption, business investment, and government spending. The second major objective of fiscal and monetary policy is to bring about a mix that corresponds generally to society's preferences.

It has been the burden of this essay that if a society wishes to have rapid growth it will have to divert a part of its output from current consumption to investment. This means that if aggregate demand is deficient, policy should aim to fill the gap with a strong dose of investment. If demand is excessively strong, policy should aim at cutting back noninvestment expenditures more sharply than plant and equipment outlays. If aggregate demand is just right, it may be necessary to build up investment at the expense of other uses of output and, at the same time, provide the corresponding saving either by creating incentive to save in the private economy or by generating a government budget surplus.

If society wishes temporarily to push its growth rate above the "natural" rate, an additional problem arises. The investment to support growth will run into diminishing profitability; extra investment now reduces the incentive to invest next year or the year after. Without luck and care, the consequence may be not only a relapse of the growth rate—which may not be so important, after all—but a shortage of total demand

and the emergence of temporary slack and unemployment.

The policy tools for operating on the composition of output are pretty clear. There are many ways of reducing or increasing taxes: Investment credits and corporate tax concessions sweeten the return on investment, and increases are likely to put pressure on plant and equipment plans. Easy credit conditions and low interest rates are likely to favor investment, because financing becomes easier and because anything that reduces the return on alternative assets is likely to make capital goods look better. Restrictive monetary policy, in reverse, is likely to contract demand mainly by decreasing the attractiveness of long-lived investments.

All this is fairly clear in principle. In fact there are two unsettled problems. The first is that different people place different values on growth as an objective of policy. It is not easy to see how any delicate consensus can be struck.

The second difficulty is a matter of "economic engineering." We have very little experience with managing the rate of investment through tax and monetary means. In 1961, fixed investment was 9.0 percent of GNP; no more could be expected in a slack economy with plenty of idle capacity. Considerations like those discussed here led the Kennedy Administration to propose the 7 percent investment credit as part of the Revenue Act of 1962; indeed, as first proposed the credit would have been a more precise instrument for stimulating marginal investment. Other, similarly intended actions were undertaken on both the fiscal and monetary fronts.

The result was that fixed investment rose to 9.2 percent of GNP in 1962 and 1963! So small an increase might have been expected simply as a result of the gradual reduction in unemployment and excess capacity, even in the absence of any deliberate intent to stimulate investment. Doubts accumulated as to whether any such policy could succeed without intolerable government interference in the private economy. But in 1964 the investment ratio rose to 9.6 percent, and in 1965 to 10.3 percent, reminiscent of the investment boom of the mid-fifties. Forecasts suggest that 1966 may be even a bigger year for fixed investment.

Does this reflect simply the luck of the game, the revival of confidence, the expectation of continued prosperity and/or inflation? Or does it mean that policies aimed at stimulating investment work with a fairly long lag, especially when they have to overcome an aversion to risk fostered by long years of economic slack? It will take a few more years of observation before anyone can know.

INDEX

ABOUT THE AUTHORS

WALTER W. HELLER, Regents' Professor of Economics at the University of Minnesota, was chairman of the President's Council of Economic Advisers from 1961 to 1964 and is presently a consultant to the Executive Office of the President. He is the author of *Taxes and Fiscal Policy in Under-Developed Countries, State Income Tax Administration* (co-author), *Savings in the Modern Economy* (co-editor), and *New Dimensions of Political Economy.*

George L. Perry is Professor of Economics at the University of Minnesota, and a consultant to the President's Council of Economic Advisers. Formerly he was Senior Economist on the Council and consultant to the President's Automation Commission.

Arthur M. Okun is chairman of the President's Council of Economic Advisers and is the author of several articles and the editor of a book, *The Battle Against Unemployment, An Introduction to a Current Issue of Public Policy.*

Warren L. Smith was chairman of the University of Michigan's Department of Economics from 1963 to 1967 and has been a consultant to several government agencies, including the Treasury Department, the President's Council of Economic Advisers, and the Anti-Trust Division of the Department of Justice. He was a senior staff member of the Council of Economic Advisers from 1962 to 1963.

James Tobin, Sterling Professor of Economics at Yale University, was a member of the President's Council of Economic Advisers from 1961 to 1962, a member of the National Advisory Committee of the Institute for Research on Poverty at the University of Wisconsin, and is chairman of the Ford Foundation's Panel on Income Minima.

Professor *Richard N. Cooper* of Yale University was on the staff of the President's Council of Economic Advisers from 1961 to 1963, and from 1965 to 1966 was Deputy Assistant Secretary of State for International Monetary Affairs. His publications include *The Economics of Interdependence: Economic Policy in the Atlantic Community.*

Robert J. Lampman is Professor of Economics at the University of Wisconsin. He is a former staff member of the President's Council of Economic Advisers (1962–63) and is the author of several books.

William G. Bowen is Provost of Princeton University. From 1964 to 1966 he was Director of Graduate Studies at Woodrow Wilson School of Public and International Affairs at Princeton. Professor Bowen is the author of *Economic Aspects of Education: Three Essays,* and *A Performing Art: Economic Dilemma* (with W. J. Baumol).

An economist at The RAND Corporation, *Richard R. Nelson* served on the staff of the President's Council of Economic Advisers from 1961 to 1963 and is the author, with Merton J. Peck and Edward D. Kalachek, of the recently published *Technology, Economic Growth and Public Policy.*

Robert M. Solow, Professor of Economics at Massachusetts Institute of Technology since 1950, was president of the Econometric Society in 1964 and is the author of several books. He was with the President's Council of Economic Advisers from 1961 to 1962.